The Men in White Coats

The Men in White Coats
Cricket Umpires Past and Present

Teresa McLean

With an Introduction by E. W. Swanton

Stanley Paul
London Melbourne Auckland Johannesburg

© Teresa McLean 1987
© Introduction E. W. Swanton 1987

All rights reserved

This edition first published in 1987 by Stanley Paul & Co Ltd,
an imprint of Century Hutchinson Ltd, Brookmount House, 62–65
Chandos Place, London WC2N 4NW

Century Hutchinson Australia (Pty) Ltd,
PO Box 496, 16–22 Church Street, Hawthorn, Melbourne, Victoria
3122

Century Hutchinson New Zealand Limited
PO Box 40–086, 32–34 View Road, Glenfield, Auckland 10

Century Hutchinson South Africa (Pty) Ltd
PO Box 337, Bergvlei 2012, South Africa

Printed and Bound in Great Britain by Anchor Brendon Ltd,
Tiptree, Essex

British Library Cataloguing in Publication Data

McLean, Teresa
    The men in white coats: cricket umpires
    past and present.
    1. Cricket—Umpiring—History
    I. Title
    796.35'83'09   GV924

ISBN 0–09–166500–0

To Martin

Contents

Acknowledgements   viii
Introduction by E. W. Swanton   ix
Author's Preface   9
1   The First Umpires   17
2   The Power of Patronage   24
3   Enter the Establishment   36
4   From Hambledon to London   49
5   The Round-arm Controversy   65
6   'Character' Umpires   77
7   The Age of Grace   94
8   The Birth-pains of Over-arm   108
9   The International Game   123
10 The Quiet Old Days   136
11 The Modern Game   151
    Index   170

Acknowledgements

The author would like to thank Jim, Richard, Mrs Paddon, Stephen Green, John Goodbody and many others.

The author and publishers also wish to thank the following for permission to reproduce illustrations:

Text Illustrations
Mary Evans Picture Library, page 103; Illustrated London News, pages 133 and 138/139; Punch Publications, pages 14, 26, 41, 57, 66, 96, 105, 132, 152, 162 and 165

Photographic Section
BBC Hulton Picture Library, pages 1 *below*, 2 *below* and 6 *below*; Patrick Eagar, pages 5 *above left, above right, below left and below right*, 7 *above and below* and 8; Illustrated London News, page 2 *above right*; Photo Source, pages 3 *above left, above right, below left and below right* and 4 *above and below left*; Press Association, page 6 *above left and above right*; Tate Gallery, London, page 1 *above*

Introduction

The quantity and variety of cricket books may well be a recurring source of wonder, but there is little, as a rule, that is surprising about each individual writer or subject. This one however is undeniably different, an attempt at a history of umpires – a novel theme attempted by a highly improbable author. Let me introduce her, though I fear she will not thank me for doing so.

One evening in the middle 1970s after talking to the Cambridge University Cricket Society I met Teresa McLean who had been one of the audience and about whose background I already knew a little. She had read history at Lady Margaret Hall and been viva'd for a First. She had played cricket for Oxford against Cambridge and in her first year taken eight for 45 – perhaps the proudest achievement of her life. She had taken herself off to India to work for Mother Teresa's Sisters of Charity in Bombay. In six months there she developed a species of diabetes so debilitating that she lost three stone and on her return was unrecognized by her mother.

Some years later she went up to Trinity, Cambridge to research for a thesis on the medieval monastery at Ely. Thus we met. She knew by now that 'the beast' would always be close behind her, that highly virulent form of diabetes which involves the utter prostration known as hypoglycaemia. Her life then is a triumph over a handicap almost unimaginable. For the benefit of other sufferers she has described her own case in a highly-acclaimed autobiography called *Metal Jam*, so named by reason of the aftertaste left by artificial sweeteners. This she added to two previous books, *Medieval English Gardens* and *The English at Play*. She has more than dabbled in journalism, and contributed theological articles in the religious columns of *The Times*.

Married now and with an infant son to look after as well as a husband who is a Cambridge history don, she has tackled a subject on which, so far as I know, no previous book has been published. Scholars and artists in many fields far removed from cricket have been magnetized by the game, but in few can its love have survived in more extraordinary circumstances then those of Mrs Martin Brett (née McLean) who can write

As it happened I was the first person to get a blue both for Oxford and for Cambridge, which is a lightweight achievement; the standard was low. But I regard even the smallest cricket honour as priceless and I am thrilled with mine.

Teresa writes as a cricketer, and she also writes as an umpire: not any old ump, need I say, pressed haphazardly into service and white coat but one who has tackled and passed (the only woman on the course) the written part of the advanced examination of the Association of Cricket Umpires. While this book is in the hands of the printer she looks for a summer's cricket divided between playing and umpiring women's games, and also making a second attempt at standing for men's clubs in East Anglia. Her first experience in this direction as described in the Author's Preface strikes the most depressing note in the book. A wrily-humorous comment in the last chapter was clearly written from first-hand experience. Men, she says, are particularly bad at accepting an unfavourable decision from a member of the opposite sex, 'especially small men with moustaches'.

Well, it seems that the club cricketers of East Anglia are going to be given a chance to redeem themselves. So be it, and if they do not give my friend better satisfaction I shall have to indulge in some investigative journalism at their expense. They have been warned.

After all of which, you will ask, what has the author

made of her novel assignment? As a scholar and a sociologist she has researched widely, well beyond the confines of cricket literature. Having absorbed a formidable list of established authorities – of whom Ashley-Cooper, Haygarth, Nyren, Pycroft, Buckley, Altham and R.S. Rait-Kerr are but a few – she has delved into archival material, especially those of the Wealden counties but also, as the game climbed up north, the strongholds of Nottingham and Sheffield, and on into the homes of the Yorkshire and Lancashire leagues.

The early years she covers with a racy pen and a highly critical eye for the social implications of a game promoted by rich and noble patrons wherein high stakes and liquor frequently combined to spark off dispute and disorder. Those whose familiarity with the game on either side of the turn of the eighteenth century derives from *The Hambledon Men* and Mary Russell Mitford's *Our Village* must prepare themselves for a distinctly less romantic picture, a debunking almost. Where so much money hung on the result – a good deal more than depends today when one considers what is the present equivalent of 500 guineas – the pressures on umpires who in many cases were in the employ of the patrons are obvious enough. (Such of the staff as gardeners, gamekeepers, bailiffs were old cricketers hired originally for their playing skill.) In lesser matches at least 'sides combined to walk off and sit down in protest with monotonous regularity'. Medieval cricket had its rough and ready side after the habit of the times, but at least after 1787 there existed in MCC a body which was both the law-maker and appeal court in one – not that the early days on Lord's grounds were free from strife and malpractice.

The author gives a highly plausible explanation of the everlasting association between cricket and pubs. Publicans were the match-makers since beer for cricket matches (and horse-races) could be brewed free of excise duty. To the pub after the game the classes mingled whether to celebrate or console. 'The events were well attended and well-oiled.'

Who was the first named umpire? The answer is amusing enough, for it was the immortal butterfingers Thomas Waymark who, at the climax of the famous match of 1744 between England and Kent (the very first of which the full score is preserved), when the last pair were together needing 3 runs to win, was confronted by a skier, whereupon, according to James Love's poem:

> The erring ball, amazing to be told!
> Slipp'd through his outstrech'd hand and mock'd his hold.
> And now the sons of Kent compleat the Game
> And firmly fix their everlasting Fame.

Poor Waymark, a sickly fellow, Miss McLean tells us, who afterwards took to umpiring – no Chester or Bird, we may be sure. We should have more confidence perhaps in a contemporary of Waymark's, 'Mr William Austen, of The Lady and Cat in Barnaby Street, who gave his judgement with the greatest impartiality, and received the thanks of the whole body, who afterwards had an elegant entertainment at his house'.

I must resist the temptation to linger longer in the pre-Marylebone days and salute the arrival on the Lord's scene of 'Honest Will' Caldecourt. A ground-boy at the age of nine, ground bowler at fifteen, and later an all-rounder for Hampshire and the Players, he came to distinction as a bold and popular umpire, and in particular a rigid upholder of the bowling law, the Sid Buller of his day.

Caldecourt officiated in the mid-nineteenth century 'in a Napoleonic pose, wearing a tricorn hat', but the white coat soon became normal wear at least in the great matches, and with a uniform came a gradual rise in status if not for many years in financial security.

Caldecourt was followed by another famous figure, 'Bob' Thoms, 1826–1903, a man of shining character and the friend of cricketers of every degree. Thoms officiated throughout the prime of W.G. Grace, and mention of the greatest of all cricketers bids me make a reluctant but emphatic disclaimer of the picture the author draws of him as being prone to all sorts of sharp practice and 'overwhelming players and umpires alike'. Thoms was not a man to be put upon, let alone overwhelmed, and in his *Wisden* obituary Sydney Pardon goes out of his way to say that 'The Graces, as cricketers, had no more fervent admirer than Thoms.' Though W.G. sometimes overstepped the mark in minor matches I know of no contemporary assessment of his nature that does not breathe affection and respect. Doubters are advised to find a copy of Bernard Darwin's inimitable biography in Duckworth's Great Lives series wherein that hint of boyish rascality is shown in due perspective.

In earliest days umpires were inclined to be ignorant and social stresses often made impartiality difficult for them. As the game evolved, knowledge as well as respect for the laws increased, and first-class cricket came to be directed ably and impartially by retired players just as it is today. The one rider to this tribute which has *always* applied is the extreme reluctance of even the best umpires to make a moral judgement in respect of unfair play. Whether it be throwing or intimidation or the niggling gamesmanship that is so irritating today, umpires are seldom prepared to apply Laws which would land fellow-professionals into serious trouble, deprive them even of their livelihood. Even Thoms said in respect of Throwing that if they wanted the law obeyed 'you gentlemen' will have to look to it. His successors have uttered or implied the same sentiments.

The author has lightened her tale with curiosities and farcical interpretations in the humbler regions such as are to be found among the illustrations. We read of the village umpire who while giving general satisfaction was regarded 'as a little too fair for such important compe-titions as the Derbyshire Wake Cups' – 'taking into consideration the peculiarities of other umpires'. The partiality of village umpires has been an ever-lasting joke. In extreme form it is scarcely, I suppose, comical – as, for instance, for opponents of the club whose combi-nation of the vicar bowling and his sexton umpiring was said to be unbeatable.

The umpires of today and yesterday are the heroes of

this book. Alex Skelding, the inimitable humourist, earns appreciative mention, including as a sample the opening sentence of his report on his benefit: 'Play began in a biting wind before a sparse crowd.' Delicacy no doubt prevented the telling of Bill Reeves's remark when Walter Robins told him what to do with his Middlesex sweater and its badge of scimitars. Buller naturally was a prime favourite. The author underlines the unique influence on his calling of Frank Chester who between the wars, having lost an arm at Salonika, joined the first-class list as a young man of twenty-six and retained his pre-eminence for 30 years. In her last chapter on the modern game she has wisely steered clear of the threat of the instant replay, but has clearly profited from talks with 'Dicky' Bird and David Constant. She still nurses the impossible dream of umpiring a Test match!

E.W. Swanton
1987

Author's Preface

I have loved cricket since I was three years old. I used to sit on the back doorstep in the sun, helping my older brother oil his bat before playing family cricket on the lawn. Umpiring decisions in these games were made by a parliamentary hierarchy in which my parents, when we could persuade them to play, were the House of Lords and my brother, sister and I the Commons. Umpires' decisions represented the survival of the fittest and, occasionally, the triumph of authority.

My experience of umpiring since then has confirmed that impression, with the balance in favour of authority but not so far in its favour that bullying, arguing and battering by appeal are rendered futile. As I went to a school that was starved of cricket, I saw few official, card-carrying umpires until I was eighteen, except those who officiated at village matches, and at the one or two matches I watched at my brother's school. These last provided me with my first sight of serious umpires, dressed for the job and looking remote, unlike our village umpires, who smiled and made faces as they fought out decisions with the opposition.

Umpires soon became objects of fascination, and I watched Sid Buller umpire Test matches almost as keenly as I watched Ted Dexter bat, Fred Trueman bowl and John Murray keep wicket. One part of Sid Buller's charisma for me came from the fact that as an umpire he was by definition mysterious. Another part came from the trappings of his job – the long white coat with the sleeves rolled up to reveal sunburnt arms – and another part of it came from the inscrutable face topped by that central parting at which I never stopped marvelling, every hair on either side of it lying short and flat, perfectly in place.

Though I only ever saw Sid Buller on television, I knew at the time that I would never forget him. He stood out from the silent throng of his umpiring contemporaries, splendid though they were, as the essence of English first class umpiring. I wasn't at all surprised, though horribly saddened, when I heard that he had died only minutes after coming off the field for rain in the County Championship match between Warwickshire and Nottinghamshire at Edgbaston in August 1970. I had always thought he would die in the middle of a game.

Buller notwithstanding, it would be wrong to pretend that umpires interested me as much as players. They fascinated me, as they still do today, but they were not, are not and never will be exciting. They are not there to be. A raised finger is not as enjoyable to watch as a cover drive, though it is usually more important. There would be something wrong if umpires were exciting. They are more like mute gods than film stars, and the more they imprint their personality on the game the more I feel uneasy about them.

My interest in cricket became really serious in the 'quiet umpires' era of the 1950s and 1960s, when Buller was the sovereign of unobtrusive authority. I did not get a glimpse of a 'character umpire' above village cricket level until I went to Oxford in 1969 when, having joined the University Women's Cricket Club just for fun, I was amazed to find myself chosen to play for them.

The standard of skill was abysmal and my knockabout games in the garden at home were enough to get me a fairly regular place in the team. More than that, being a potential female Botham with a talent for trouble, I was chosen to play in the Varsity match. Writing this now, I am ashamed to say that I cannot remember how the game turned out, but I rather think we won. I remember most things about it vividly, including the weather, the setting, the way I was out (run out) and the umpires.

We played in pouring rain on a pitch lent us by one of the mens' colleges, miles down the Botley Road. It was more of a meadow than a cricket field, though it did have something approaching a pavilion – a grim little shed in which we sheltered when lightning stopped play. We did not have a set uniform and wore whites which ranged from jeans to shorts and, horror of horrors, divided skirts. There was nothing to distinguish Oxford from Cambridge, and team identity depended on us knowing each other.

I reckoned my forte was my unusual spin bowling, but my captain unwisely ignored this hidden talent and left me out of the bowling attack, so it was up to my batting to vindicate my selection. I went in at number seven. The storm was immediately overhead, with thunder cracking round the ground, and we had nearly got the total we were chasing. There was no point hanging around: I launched some uninhibited shots, made a quick little clutch of runs, then was run out when I slipped in the mud attempting a suicidal run.

The umpire, I remember, stood in the rain with his collar up, shook his head and said 'Out!'. As I walked past him he added, 'Silly girl.' As far as I was concerned, coming from an umpire who looked authoritative, had the keys to the shed, was a man, and was standing in the Varsity match, that was 'character umpiring'. It made a deep impression on me.

Cricket then was even more sexist than it is today, difficult though that might be to imagine. We almost always played mens' teams because there were hardly any womens' teams. Once we played a prep school about fifteen miles outside Oxford and it was peculiarly humiliating to be given out by a small, spotty boy. Thank heavens there is genuine women's first class cricket today, with women umpiring. Maybe one day I will be able to fulfil my ambition, though I know it is only a dream, to umpire a Test match.

It was when I had left Oxford and come back from

India, where I worked for Mother Teresa's Sisters in Bombay, that my attitude to umpires changed, moving from passive fascination to active interest. In India I did not take advantage of the chance to see amateur umpires giving Test matches a unique charm; I was too overwhelmed by my first experience of the terrible poverty all around me to think of anything else. I didn't go to a single first class or club match in all the months I was there, though every street was the scene of a game, complete with survival-of-the-fittest umpiring by group argument reminiscent of my childhood.

I left India feeling depressed and ill and it was only when I found out I was diabetic, was treated for it and began to feel a bit better, almost a year after getting back, that I began to recover my spirits and with them my interest in cricket. I accepted a post teaching at Cheltenham Ladies College, because the job would pay the rent and because Cheltenham was one of the few girls schools in the country that played cricket. It gave up cricket the day I arrived.

I devoted my attention to the surrounding village matches, where I joined the locals in decrying the umpires as everything from racists to mental paraplegics. Umpiring is one of those occupations which is easy to get right from the sidelines. I joined a long village cricket tradition of armchair umpires and, in the same tradition, enjoyed bad umpiring as one of the adornments of the game, ripe for critical dissection, provided its faults were enigmatic and its setting idyllic.

My expectations of county cricket and county umpires were altogether different. Born and brought up in Surrey, I was a Surrey supporter, and my mental picture of the typical county umpire, confirmed by my few visits to the Oval on bleak afternoons, was brought to life by the first umpire I ever got to know at all well. In fact, though, he was a club, not a county performer. In autumn 1976 I went up to Trinity College, Cambridge to do a thesis on medieval history, and joined the Cambridge University Women's Cricket Club, whose umpire was a retired policeman. Typecast for the job, tall, dark and unexpressive, quiet and incorruptible, he became our mascot, bridging the gap between village cricket and serious club cricket and even emanating overtones of the county game.

We took ourselves reasonably seriously, helped by the seriousness with which our umpire viewed us, but we were regularly beaten by nearby villages and schools. Men's colleges helped us sharpen our attitude by playing us left- or one-handed. Through it all our umpire stood like a rock in the ocean, sustaining us with his reticence.

Our Cambridge team was keener than the Oxford team had been, and towards the end of my first year we went across to Oxford full of fighting spirit and stories of past Oxford outrages and umpiring crimes. We played the 1977 Varsity on the Wadham College pitch, on a lovely sunny day. It was nice to be back in Oxford and I felt I couldn't lose. Our umpire stood as straight and cryptic as ever, even when we won, and only revealed afterwards how pleased he was by eating a chocolate someone offered him and smiling a rare smile.

For me it was a glorious match. I was the first woman ever to get a Blue for both Oxford and Cambridge, though since I was a woman they were only half blues. I bowled 15.4 overs and took 8 for 45. The rest of the team stood in a huddle on the grass afterwards and elected me captain for the next year. I wished women were as clubby as men so we could have taken our umpire out to dinner, but we contented ourselves with melting away in triumph, our umpire sitting bolt upright on his coach seat, fast asleep.

The following year, 1978, I got a sudden attack of feminist fury at the prospect of having to play the Varsity match on a second-rate ground again. As it was our turn to be the hosts, I asked the Cambridge groundsman, the marvellous Cyril Coote, for permission to play at Fenners. He agreed without a moment's hesitation, prepared a pitch such as none of us had ever played on before, and stayed all through the game to watch us grow to fit the glory allotted us. I think umpires are as much affected by their cricketing surroundings as

13

Bowler. "WOULD YOU MIND STANDING SIDEWAYS OLD CHAP?"
Umpire. "I WILL–BUT IT'S WORSE."

players. In the Fenners game we became more reveren-
tial towards our two umpires, who in their turn became
visibly more stately.

That one match at Fenners is the only time I have
ever taken part in a game on a really good ground.
When I left Cambridge, however, I took what could be
construed as the first faltering steps towards doing so

again: I went to ACU evening classes to learn to qualify as an umpire.

The classes were in a school gym miles out along one of the minor roads of West Oxford, which was where I lived; I had gone back there to teach. They were extremely well taught by an exact and dedicated man, the model fanatical umpire, but I had not expected thirty people to turn up week after week to listen to his talks, look at the ground plans he drew on his blackboard and the little magnetic feet he moved about on a magnetic sketch of a pitch to explain no-ball decisions.

At the end of an eight-week term came the exams, set each year by the Association of Cricket Umpires. There were two levels of examination, depending on the grade of game one wanted to umpire. The easier one would have qualified me to umpire local club and village matches, but I had big ideas and opted for the harder exam, which would qualify me to umpire any level of match, right up to Test match standard, subject to the usual requirements of experience and performance. I was the only woman who took the harder exam and one of only two women who took either.

I passed, the exam having an 80 per cent passmark, and the following year, when I married and moved back to Cambridge, I started to umpire for the East Anglian club circuit. My first game was ghastly. I was nervous, and was alternately showered with abuse and advice by the men over whom I was supposed to be asserting my authority. My authority anyway was minimal, regarded sceptically by the players and going from weak to moribund with every bad and hesitant decision I made. I gave one particularly unpleasant little man run out: he was out by a good four yards.

He stood staring at me and said, 'Are you seriously trying to give me out?'

When I said I was, he retorted, 'Well, I'm not going.'

I looked at my watch and told him he had two minutes to get off the field and let the next man in: they were ticking away. Thank God, he went. I had no idea what I'd have done had he refused, and I decided umpiring was one of the most unpleasant jobs in the world. In future I would have as little to do with it as possible.

I daresay a new season will change my mind, but in the meantime I am happy playing for Cambridge Ladies, umpiring and scoring the odd over when I am free. It is just as well, because shortly after I arrived in Cambridge I took the ACU oral exam that accompanies the written exam, and failed it. I had not done nearly enough homework, my small son was galloping around outside making chaos, and I lacked the two years' experience recommended as a necessary preparation.

This coming summer I intend to overcome my inhibitions about umpiring mens' matches, accumulate one good year of the two years' necessary experience and resuscitate my Test match dream. You never know. Cricket is full of surprises.

The nicest surprise it has produced for me recently is the chance to do this book. Writing it has plunged me into a wealth of umpiring lore, stories and traditions which I knew must exist but have only just discovered in their full, delightful, eccentric richness. It has made umpires and umpiring a love as well as a fascination.

1

The First Umpires

The most powerful participants in a cricket match are the umpires. They are the only ones on the field all through the game; the only ones who can determine the course of the game at any time; the only ones whose every gesture and utterance is significant. Umpiring is the perfect job for anyone hungry for power and reluctant to expose himself to the uncertainties and humiliations of playing. The only pressure an umpire has to face is that his decisions may, once in a while, be wrong; but he can go on making them with impunity as long as the match lasts. He is the non-playing monarch of cricket.

Umpiring has not always been like that. Umpires are almost as old as cricket but they have not had an easy ride. Cricket has become more complex and more elaborately regulated over the years, and umpiring has become correspondingly more complicated and burdened with rules. At least nowadays umpires are less likely to be killed trying to enforce them. They are there to conduct the game according to its laws, where once they were there to haggle with the players about the rules, to prevent brawling, and to try to see the game to a peaceful end. Cricket is a polite shadow of the wild and violent sport it once was and umpires have been the first to benefit from this.

Some sort of bat and ball game with a wicket and fielders has probably always been played, but the first clearly identifiable cricket games date from the late seventeenth, early eighteenth century, and at that time

17

umpires only appear occasionally in the records, as last resorts.

Before that, during the Puritan commonwealth, cricket was mainly a boys' street game, and the only official records that showed any interest in it were court rolls, which condemned it for keeping people away from church. Almost all incidental references to cricket are hostile and all associate it with violence and drinking, features which distinguished the game for the next two hundred years. In 1672 a religious stalwart called George Swinnocke wrote:

> Maidstone was formerly a very profane town, insomuch that [before 1640] I have seen morris-dancing, cudgel playing, stool-ball, cricket, and many other sports played openly and publicly on the Lord's Day.

The nearest figure to an umpire in those early days of street cricket must have been the occasional sympathetic onlooker who helped organise the game. In 1622 five boys were hauled up before the magistrates at Boxgrove, near Chichester, for playing cricket during evening prayer time on a Sunday 'after sufficient warnings given to the contrary'. Their offence was particularly heinous because the churchwardens, Richard Martin, father of one of the players, and Thomas West 'defended and maintained them in it'. The churchwardens were not exactly umpires, probably somewhere between supporters, umpires and look-outs, apparently they did not stop the boys breaking the church windows and nearly beating a child's brains out with their bats.

Seventeenth-century coroners' reports often mention cricket as a cause of violent death, and it became obvious that the game needed some form of mediator or *umpire* – (old english numpere, non-pair) – a neutral in the contest, called in to settle differences. Seventeenth-century literature is full of references to umpires; not cricket umpires but arbiters in all sorts of disputes: between king and parliament, rival lovers, rival nations, happy and sad natures, prosecution and defence at law, and so on.

The fewer the laws, the more important, and contro-

18

versial, the umpires. By the early 1700s a body of cricket lore and commonly accepted principles seems to have evolved, but it is not at all clear that there were written laws, and, if there were, they clearly left a lot of points open to argument. Even after a body of basic cricket law was more or less accepted everywhere by the mid-eighteenth century, it did not provide consistent answers to contentious questions.

Umpires were just as likely to cause as to settle trouble. On points where the ruling varied from club to club and village to village, or on points where the law had not been worked out or had been recently or locally changed, or where the existing law was unpopular, their decisions could hardly avoid being sources of dispute.

Drink was one of the factors which often turned disputes into riots or battles. During the civil war cricket became a popular pastime with bored landowners living on their estates, and with the Restoration it came into its own as a fashionable sport in London as well as the countryside. It kept its rough and ready side, but developed a fashionable and aristocratic side too; every serious team had both sorts of player and they celebrated or consoled themselves about the match by drinking together. Drink was intrinsic to cricket.

Matches were usually arranged and sponsored by publicans. The Ram at Smithfield was a favourite haunt of noblemen wishing to show off their sporting enthusiasm by sponsoring cricket matches in London, and in 1668 it was rated as a cricket-field for the first time, because its owner brewed beer for the games he arranged on his fields at Clerkenwell. Brewers providing beer for special occasions like cricket matches and horse races did not have to pay excise duty, the beer was cheap and the events were well-attended and well-oiled.

By the late seventeenth century cricket was popular enough to get coverage in newspapers, usually in the form of advertisements for matches, and these were usually put in by inn-keepers. They announced the prize to be played for and the teams which would be playing.

One of the earliest newspaper adverts for a match appeared in *The Post Boy* for 28 to 30 March 1700:

> These are to inform gentlemen, or others, who delight in cricket playing, that a match at cricket, of 10 gentlemen on each side, will be played on Clapham Common, near Foxhall, on Easter Monday next, for £10 a head each game (five being design'd) and £20 the odd one.

Typical London cricket of the time: short – five games planned for the day; gentlemanly; unconcerned with the weather – matches were often played in spring and autumn; generously endowed, and as readily played with ten as with eight, nine or eleven players. There was no mention of an ordinary, or feast, after the match, probably because it was a series of short matches and there would be too many players to entertain, but the ordinary soon became part of every serious cricket fixture, a mainstay of the close relationship between cricket, pubs, eating and drinking. It always took place after the game; drinking went on before, during and after the game, which might start as early as nine or ten o'clock in the morning.

The other big force for excitement in cricket was gambling, which was the life-blood of the game. Pretty well every match, however humble, was heavy with bets. The very first recorded cricket match, at Coxheath, Kent, in 1646, produced a court case which centred on the non-payment of a gambling debt. All this was bound to have the most alarming double effect on umpires. Obviously umpires were indispensable for settling disputes and laying down the law. But that meant they were to blame for every expensive decision, and with everyone gambling, every decision was expensive for someone.

> This day was played a match in the White Conduit Fields for a considerable sum of money, between the Men of Kent and the Men of London. The Kentish Men won the wager. (*The Postman*, 19 August 1719)

Early village cricket had no reason to keep written records of its games, so we know nothing about its accompanying beers and bets. Where records do exist they are brutally bare, like this entry in the diary of a Kentish farmer: 'Memorandum, ye 23 June 1708. Wee beat Ash Street at Creckits.'

Advertisements for more sizeable fixtures usually mentioned the prizes offered: a hat for every player in the winning team was a common one. But the prizes were as nothing next to the bets. The stakes for which games were to be played were proudly advertised in local papers, of which there was a growing number in the early eighteenth century, and when it was a really big match, the stakes were advertised in the national papers. Years before the aristocracy and gentry were playing cricket, they were betting on it. By the mid-eighteenth century, when cricket was a fashionable game, even the most undistinguished teams and their umpires could be vehicles for gambling on a prodigious scale by local aristocrats. In his famous account of the early Hambledon Club, Nyren says they always played for stakes of at least £500.

It was the development of cricket into a big gambling game that improved cricketing records. Bets were not restricted to the results of games; they covered individual performances too, and some sort of score-card was essential for recording these.

The first explicit reference we have to an umpire in the early cricket records is in a poem called 'In Certamen Pilae', written and published in 1706 by an old Etonian who went to King's College, Cambridge, William Goldwin. It is an account of an imaginary game but accurately reflects the new popularity of cricket with gentry, arrivistes and the prosperous middle class. To give it the desired air of gentility, Goldwin wrote it in Latin, with a parallel text in English. It does not mention betting as such, but it gives an effective picture of an early umpire arbitrating cricket disputes under the pressures of a big game, one of which was almost always gambling.

. . . Then quarrels rife, while all exclaim,
And all would lord it o'er the game.
Now some grey veteran intercedes
And wins their love, the while he pleads:
A Daniel come to judgement, he
To all around speaks equity . . .
rich is he in cricket lore . . .
And proves that they need strive no more

Umpires have never had a scintillating image; they have always been cast as the grey-haired elder statesman Goldwin portrayed so tediously. Primitive cricket may have started with only one umpire a game; there is no way of knowing, but all the early references to umpires, including this one, mention two.

Each at his wicket, near at hand,
Propped on his staff, the umpires stand.

Grey-haired image notwithstanding, the umpires' chief function, of settling arguments before they got to the stage of physical violence and crowd intervention, could be a strenuous one. In 1715 William Waterfall, a Derbyshire man and one of a big cricketing family of Waterfalls, was convicted of manslaughter because he killed his opponent in a cricket match. Early pictures of umpires show them dressed for the Daniel-in-judgement role rather than the riot policeman role, wearing ostentatiously formal clothes, with three-cornered hats and dark knee breeches, leaning on staves. The batsmen had to hit these staves with their bats to score notches, and the staves were usually the long, curved bats used by cricketers at the time. It is a fair assumption that at least some of the spectators shown in any picture of an eighteenth century cricket match are bookies offering odds on who would score the most notches, and the rest of the crowd are punters.

Cricket in the early eighteenth century was concentrated in London, Hampshire and the south-east, Kent in particular. Village, club and county cricket was now popular with all classes, not just with the 'citizens and peasants' a seventeenth-century observer had seen playing it. Indeed, so popular and fashionable had cricket become that in 1710 Queen Anne had to admit that it had come to stay, and gave it her reluctant blessing.

Cricket is not illegal, for it is a very MANLY game – not bad in itself but only in the ill-use of it by betting more than £10 on it – that is bad, and against the law.

Bets, of course, were often a hundred times bigger than the £10 she set as the limit and it must have horrified poor, well meaning Queen Anne that, umpires and players as well as spectators laid bets. Umpires were not officially banned from betting until 1835, and even then there was no way of enforcing the prohibition. The complexities of cricket law and custom, gambling and umpiring were impenetrable, but players, punters and umpires went on gambling regardless.

2

The Power of Patronage

Early eighteenth-century cricket was a full-blooded financial brawl patronised by aristocrats, bookies, publicans and the socially and locally ambitious. These were the people who appointed umpires.

By the early 1730s cricket clubs abounded in the south of England. Some villages, such as Henfield in Sussex, and some London suburbs which were then villages, such as Mitcham, Surrey, kept records of their games and occasionally, when there was enough trouble to warrant it, records of their umpires. Country house cricket offered better grounds and the most splendid entertainments. London cricket went from strength to strength. Its big grounds, like the Artillery Ground at Finsbury, just outside the city, attracted enormous crowds and a wealth of journalists, bookies and food and drink stalls.

Cricket had enough stature to offer umpires a considerable reputation if they emerged with credit from the tangle of problems endemic in the game, of which the greatest was the dependence of umpires on patrons. This was true whatever the class of cricket played. Social patronage could be just as strong in villages as on great estates, though it was more complicated; village umpires standing for the odd game now and then might risk losing work, custom or friendship from the people they offended. There was no such thing as an independent umpire.

A lot of the qualities required of umpires have been the same from the early days to the present, but there were some qualities specially required by early cricket and they only make sense if we can make sense of the game itself, which was a simple and robust affair embellished with innumerable local variations.

The earliest surviving set of rules for a cricket match was put together on 11 July 1727 and gives a vivid, not to say bloodthirsty, picture of country house cricket at that time. The rules are for a game played by the Duke of Richmond's team and a team belonging to a Mr Brodrick of Pepperharrow, near Godalming in Surrey. They are a manifesto of early cricket, and are graphic on the subject of umpires' problems. They are not a complete set of laws, but a summary of additions and alterations to the basic laws already in existence, whether these were written or oral, which is uncertain.

The Duke of Richmond was the grandson of Charles II and took pride in declaring himself the first aristocrat to play as well as promote cricket. He was one of a small group of influential patrons who firmly established cricket as a fashionable game in the south of England. John Sidney, the Earl of Leicester, sponsored matches at Penshurst, including one of the first county matches, between Kent and Sussex, in 1728. The Sackvilles at Knole took a pugnacious part in the rivalry between great houses nearby, until Lord John Sackville went off his head in the 1750s.

Early aristocratic cricket seems to have had an inordinately high casualty rate. Frederick Prince of Wales was a passionate cricketer until he died in 1751, of an abcess caused by a blow from a cricket ball. Before that he followed with keen interest the fortunes of his friend the Duke of Richmond, who managed to stay healthy and sane. There was a tight circuit of aristocratic rivalry and big matches were great occasions for gossip and political plotting. The Duke's other great rival, Sir William Gage, was the M.P. for Seaford, which lay under the Duke's jurisdiction as Lord High Constable of England, and the two played out their political rivalries on the cricket field.

Though not a titled member of the circuit, Mr Brodrick was a substantial landowner and played

"He's either signalling leg-byes or he wants five-to-four on the favourite."

enough cricket against the Duke for their matches to be important events. One of the local peculiarities in this game was that they played with twelve men in each team. Eleven seems to have been the usual number, though nine, ten and even fourteen were common.

The scale of the gambling on this game is impossible to calculate, but it would have been extremely eccentric for two such well set-up teams to have contented themselves with playing for the prize money of a guinea a head. It was so unusual for gentlemen to play without gambling that one cricket club advertised for gentlemen members by boasting its distinguishing feature: it played the game 'for diversion only', *i.e.* not for bets. The Duke of Richmond was not one of the 'diversion only' minority.

He got his team together by means which every aristocratic patron used: he hired any good players he found as members of his estate staff. During the season they played for his side and during the winter they did the jobs to which they had been appointed: gardener, stableman, bailiff, gamekeeper. The Duke's seat at Goodwood was famous for its cricketing staff.

The 1727 game against Mr Brodrick's team was to be the first of two matches: one in Surrey, on a ground to be chosen by Mr Brodrick; the other a month later, on a ground to be chosen by the Duke.

The thorny question of who should choose the umpires and who they should be was solved in classic eighteenth-century style: the Duke appointed one umpire, Mr Brodrick appointed the other. It was a pragmatic acknowledgement of the balance of power between umpires and patrons. The balance was in favour of the patrons, but even they could not openly change umpires' decisions, only put them under gruesome pressure which could, occasionally, be resisted. Richard Nyren, whose son later wrote the classic 'The Young Cricketer's Tutor', inspired his son to raptures with his heroic resistance to patronal pressure.

> I have known him maintain an opinion with great firmness against the Duke of Dorset and Sir Horace Mann, and when, in consequence of his being proved to be in the right, the latter has afterwards crossed the ground and shaken him heartily by the hand.

The fact that this exhibition of heroism took place while Richard Nyren was playing as well as umpiring was less important than the heroism itself and the possibilities it opened up for fair umpiring.

Big matches often used gentleman umpires because they were thought to be less vulnerable to financial manipulation. Richard Nyren was a gentleman, though that does not diminish his fortitude in standing up to an infamous pair of thugs like the Duke of Dorset and Sir Horace Mann. The trouble was that in a match like the 1727 one there was no way of stopping the bullying, and the bribery could be more subtle than the offering of money; a friend, no matter how gentlemanly, would be susceptible to a wide variety of social pressures and embarrassments.

The hold patrons had over umpires is stated with horrible clarity in article twelve of the agreement Richmond and Mr Brodrick drew up.

> If any doubt or dispute arises on any of the aforesaid articles, or whatever else is not settled therein, it shall be determined by the Duke of Richmond and Mr Brodrick on their honours, by whom the umpires are likewise to be determined on any difference between them.

We are spared the details of how the Duke of Richmond and Mr Brodrick were to resolve *their* disputes.

In return for playing the part demanded of them, the umpires were protected by their patrons from intimidation by anyone else on the field of play. 'If any of the gamesters shall speak or give their opinion on any point of the game, they are to be turned out, and voided in the match.' Presumably by a bunch of the patrons' heavies. There then follows the saving clause: 'This not to extend to the Duke of Richmond and Mr Brodrick.'

The obvious implication of the Duke's and Mr Brodrick's prohibition of both speaking and giving an opinion about an umpire's decision is that opinions were often given by more robust methods than speaking.

Intimidation of umpires could reach dramatic heights. Country house cricket was not known for its gentility. Four years after his game against Mr Brodrick, the Duke of Richmond and his team were attacked by a mob at Richmond because they arrived late and then wasted time, so that their cricketing and gambling opponents did not have a chance to win. The crowd took a dim view of it and the Duke, his team and his umpires were lucky to escape with their lives. Fines for riot and battery were commonplace.

Often there was no way of roping the crowd off at village matches, and it was common for spectators to pour onto the pitch during the game, giving advice, making observations and threats, and helping umpires to make decisions. Some pictures from quite an early date show crowds kept at a distance, but that was rare.

We do not know the names of the umpires who had to stand in the Richmond/Brodrick game, nor do we know any other personal facts about them. The rules do not say whether the umpires got a match fee, a compensation fee for their trials, or help with their expenses. Umpires' pay has been a sore point with umpires since the game began and it would be nice to think that in this case, as friends of the match organisers, they were included in the ordinary afterwards, as long as they had not put their well-being at risk with foolishly fair-minded decisions.

Cricket ordinaries were careless of class, even in a magnificent setting like Goodwood. They usually provided huge sides of beef, meat pies and bottomless supplies of beer, to be consumed by everyone who had played in the game, whatever his status. This was followed by singing, sometimes with an impromptu recital or ditty about the winning shot or the glories of the winning team. I have never seen an early cricket song that mentioned an umpire. They have never been very inspiring figures.

The game they supervised was different from the modern game in some striking respects. It was, for example, a bowler's game. A score of twenty was often a winning score and though bowling at the time of the Richmond/Brodrick game was all along the ground – rolling, it was often called – balls were constantly rocketing off the pitch.

Pitches were usually shorn of long grass, but only by hand; they were not closely mown, and a really evil pitch could be the key to success. Pitching was a prized art. Generally the visiting team chose the pitch because it was too great an advantage for the home captain to do so, being familiar with every bump, pit and growth that might help his bowlers. When home captains did choose the pitch, there was usually a return match on the opposition's ground, to give them the advantage in their turn.

The Duke of Richmond and Mr Brodrick took it in turns to choose the pitch, but not personally; the Duke's umpire chose when they played in Sussex and Mr Brodrick's umpire chose when they played in Surrey. 'The pitches shall be pitched in a fair and even place', announced one of the articles, though the only people who could enforce that were the Duke and Mr Brodrick, who could always sabotage fair play by getting their umpires to choose pitches with treacherous secrets for their teams to exploit.

Twenty years later it had become more common for the toss for innings to carry with it the choice of pitch, and umpires often did the tossing and choosing. Umpires and pitches took up no less than five of the sixteen points covered in the 1727 articles of agreement.

There was a whole catalogue of names for the effects of raw pitches on underarm bowling, especially when it was all along the ground; bouncing bowling was only just beginning to replace rolling. Even when it had become common practice, by the 1750s, the pitch still had dire effects; if anything, worse than before. Among the triumphs of a rough pitch were:

a didapper – a ball that bounced twice,

a ground ball – one that hit the ground three times or more,

a shooter – one that suddenly flew up after hitting a lump.

The batsman's only weapon against this sort of attack was the long, thin stick which he used as a bat and held without gloves. Underarm rolling and bowling could be fast; on bad pitches it could be frighteningly fast. The advent of bouncing bowling led to the use of wider, straight bats in the 1750s, and with them came progress towards a more even balance between batting and bowling.

In 1727 the batsmen needed all the help they could get. Richmond and Brodrick chose the ball or balls to be used. Early cricket balls were hand sewn and were of extremely variable quality; some games were played with balls that had to be pushed back in their skins every time they got loose. Precautionary ball changes were declared out of the umpires' control in this particular game, though often the umpires did control the use of balls, usually by marking the one used at the start of the game so they would notice if it was changed. There was the usual wrangling to be gone through if the captain of the bowling side wanted to give his bowlers a boost by changing to a dangerously decrepit ball.

In all early cricket an umpire's main responsibility towards batsmen was to stand where they could touch his staff with their bats to score notches (runs). That is why the umpire at the batsman's end is shown in all cricket pictures right up until the early nineteenth century standing at leg slip, where his staff was in easy reach, not at square leg, to which position he gratefully retreated when staff touching stopped being the means of scoring notches.

Short notches were favourite causes of dispute and it took a brave umpire to call one if he thought the batsman had not run the full length of the pitch. Notches and short notches were signalled to the notchers, or scorers, who sat on the field of play with long hazel sticks into which they cut a notch for every run scored and a deep notch for every fifth or every tenth run, to make adding up easier at the end.

The notchers, like the umpires, retreated gradually as batting improved, until they reached their present position outside the boundary ropes. In 1727 there were, as yet, no boundaries. Every notch had to be run and the number of notches scored could be shouted to the notchers without a signal. Long after the introduction of the popping crease, batsmen continued to hit the umpire's staff to score a notch. The fact that the Duke and Mr Brodrick made staff touching one of their rules suggests that the custom was already being abandoned by some teams and its use in this game therefore needed written confirmation.

The popping crease in its original form was one of the game's many afflictions, and it was one that caused more distress to wicket-keepers than batsman. Until the mid-eighteenth century, while bats were still long, thin and curved, a running batsman was considered to be 'in' if he managed to get the end of his bat into a hole in the ground in front of the stumps, specially cut for the purpose, before the poor, gloveless keeper managed to pop the ball into it.

The tally of broken and mutilated hands resulting from this practice was too grisly and the popping hole was replaced by a popping crease, first cut and later painted into the turf. Another theory about the origin of the name popping crease is that the crease was the place where the batsman popped, or tapped, the umpire's staff. Either way, its introduction was a welcome improvement. Wicket-keeping became a more popular job.

Breaking the wicket with ball in hand was another dangerous manoeuvre and one on which the Duke and Mr Brodrick insisted if a run out was to be claimed. Theirs was a traditional stance. Plenty of people at the time played that it was enough to throw the wicket down; putting it down with ball in hand was unnecessary. Run outs have always been hair-raising for umpires, who must have been glad when the 'thrown' run out was universally accepted, if only because it was easier to see what was happening without two bodies, at least one of them travelling at top speed, obscuring their view of the ball.

The run out by throwing was slow to evolve into general use. Long after it entered the laws as a legal method of dismissal, in 1755, purists could hardly bring themselves to count 'thrown out' as a real dismissal. Score-cards did not mention the name of the fielder responsible for a run out, and when names did start to appear, in the 1770s, the scorers differentiated between thrown out and run out, and continued to do so until well into the nineteenth century. As late as 1893 Rev. W. K. R. Bedford wrote in the *English Illustrated Magazine* 'Yet even in my recollection we scarcely thought a batsman properly run out unless the wicket was put down by the hand.'

It has never been easy to run, put or throw a batsman out, and the Richmond/Brodrick game not only insisted on the ball being in hand for a run out but also had wickets made of only two stumps; thin, miserable sticks v-shaped at the top with another stick lying across them. At first wickets were low and wide, about 2″ by 1″, but they were made taller and narrower throughout the eighteenth century, until they reached their present size of 24″ by 7″ in 1788. The only difference then was that they were topped by one bail, not two.

If a fielder looked like running a batsman out, the batsman could collide with him in the interests of self, or wicket, defence. Sadly, the only details of dismissals given in most early score-cards are the bowler's name and, when applicable, the catcher's name, so we have missed out on a host of gory titbits about collisions, charges and crashes. There was a terse entry in a Sheffield score-card for a batsman who got himself out in 1792, 'run out of the ground to hinder a catch'. Worse still, a man called John Boots was killed, without any embellishment by the record writer, in a game played in 1737 between Newick and Henfield, Sussex, 'by running against another man in crossing the wicket.'

Umpires probably used their staves partly for self-defence when a game was at its height. Mayhem was bound to occur when crowds were large, financially committed to one of the teams and to players' individual performances and were, more often than not, drunk.

Some of the worst incidents occurred at single-wicket matches, which were very popular in the eighteenth, and early nineteenth centuries. These were games between anything from one to six a side, though one a side was the best loved. They were based on the same principles as children's cricket: to score a run, the batsman had to run to the bowler's end, where there was just one stump, and back to his wicket. When there were fewer than five players a side, the area behind the wicket was 'dead'.

This newspaper report of a single-wicket match played on Kennington Common in 1737, between one man from Wandsworth and one from Mitcham, shows how dangerous cricket, especially single-wicket cricket, could be.

John Smith, a mechanic, for many years a foreman to Mr Strong, a painter in Doctors Commons, died of a wound he received by a cut from a stone yesterday at the cricket match on Kennington Common, when the mob outrageously threw dirt, dung etc. . .

Injuries to players, however they happened, were dealt with in the 1727 articles of agreement, which allowed any player 'taken lame or sick after the match is begun' to be replaced and, if the captain wished, to come back when he was better. If a suitable substitute could not be

33

found, the other side had to drop one of its players until the casualty returned.

Such allowances were made in order to keep the conditions of play constant and to avoid deliberate injuries which might swing the game. Although the only substitutes allowed in the official laws were men who had already played, fresh ones were forbidden; with a lot of money staked, it was safer to regulate the game so that injuries were not profitable to either side. The usual policy with injuries was to carry on, leaving the casualties to feel sorry for themselves. With 'great bets depending', injured players could be made to feel very sorry indeed. On 31 July 1735 the *Grub Street Journal* reported that in one such game played between the Gentlemen of Chelsea and the Gentlemen of Clapham, on Clapham Common, '. . . Mr Row, one of the gamesters, broke his arm in a fall', and cost his backers a lot of money.

One of an umpire's trickiest tasks was to detect pseudo-injuries. He was also the sole judge of 'all frivolous delays, of all hurts, whether real or pretended' and of any time-wasting these might involve – a truly ghastly responsibility. If local heroes were given a hard time by umpires, crowd trouble inevitably loomed. There is a distinct touch of irony in this verse compiled by a mid-eighteenth-century cricket club about the retired players who scored and umpired their games:

> Some mark the strokes upon the shaven spray,
> And others umpires stand whom all obey.

Umpires were often old players; they knew the most about the game and were the least likely to be conned by the players. That does not mean player-umpires had a soft ride. If anything, crowds were more ferocious in their criticisms of ex-players than of casual or gentlemen umpires. In 1788 Leicester beat Coventry and the local paper reported 'a scene of bloodshed . . . scarcely to be credited in a country so entirely distinguished for acts of humanity.'

The 1727 articles also have provisions unusual enough

to keep the crowd suspicious and the umpires alert, though there is no match report to indicate how such eccentricities were received. All catches were allowed, 'clothed or not clothed', which was a controversial point. Many clubs did not allow catches that lodged in the clothing or resulted from the ball lodging in the clothing – hats were the main problem, but it looks as if their use was allowed in the 1727 game. Shirts and jackets were commonly used to catch balls right up until the early nineteenth century.

The strategic use of clothing was most controversial when the clothing concerned belonged to the batsman, who was entitled to fend off fielders if they got in his way while he was running. Fielders' efforts to take the ball out of his shirt, or wherever it had got itself trapped, might lead them to claim a catch.

Catching behind the wicket was another exceptional provision of the Richmond/Brodrick rules and one which demanded extra attention from the umpires, with the ball bouncing at odd angles towards the keeper, who stood a long way from the wicket, more like a long-stop than a keeper.

The arrangement of early cricket laws and customs was open to negotiation. That is how the game worked itself into a final, standard pattern. The umpires in the early days were the scapegoats for experiments and the sorting out of traditions. Wides, no-balls, lost balls – none of these existed in their list of duties or responsibilities, but even so players had, as they have now, a freer and easier time than umpires.

Though the game was a celebration of local pride, players did not let local allegiances cramp their style. Unlike umpires, they moved about wherever they could find a patron to take them on for a season. The Duke of Richmond's groom, who won the game for Kent against the rest of the South at Penshurst in 1729, did so by moving round the country house circuit to play a season at Penshurst. No umpire would ever find a patron to do that for him.

3

Enter the Establishment

By the 1740s London was the cricketing capital of England. The great days of eighteenth-century village cricket were great days too for club cricket in London and for club and county cricket all round the city. By mid-century a London club had drawn up the first complete set of cricket laws, which were published and accepted throughout the game, and which recognised umpires as important figures. By the end of the century the Marylebone Cricket Club was the governing body of cricket and by 1815 Thomas Lord had established his magnificent ground in its present position. London and its suburbs were rich with cricket.

It was in London that the middle class first launched into cricket in a big way. When the game became fashionable, middle class entrepreneurs poured money into cricket promotion and, increasingly, into cricket playing. London cricket was a patchwork of class divisions and class integration; of residential and seasonal cricket – middle and working class Londoners played it from the start of spring to the end of autumn, while aristocrats and landed gentlemen brought their cricket up to town in between periods in the country.

London cricket had a lively relationship with the game everywhere else, regardless of distance. 'Going against London' was a high spot of the season, especially in Kent and Surrey, where county pride was fierce, and the matches were watched with avid interest which brought out the savage in neighbourhood emotions. Villages with good cricketing reputations liked nothing better than to vindicate them with a victory against a good London side. On Monday 6 September 1742 Slindon in Sussex played 'XI picked gentlemen of London' at the Artillery Ground, Finsbury, forcing the Surrey/London match scheduled for that day to be postponed for a week.

Such was the ferocity of crowd feelings that at games like this it was dangerous to keep opposing factions waiting more than a few minutes, high on beer and bets, and visiting teams were threatened with 100 guinea fines if they arrived late.

Playing on the Artillery Ground was an honour. The ground was opened in 1724 and almost at once became the most important in London. It belonged to the exclusive London Club, whose president was the Prince of Wales, and it was the venue for all distinguished and important matches. As many as 10,000 people, a fifth of the population of London, went to its biggest games. It also hosted any extraordinary matches that might draw a good crowd, such as the one played there on 13 July 1747 between the women of Charlton, Sussex and the women of Westdean and Chilgrove, Sussex. There were quite a few womens' matches but this one was rated so highly that the standard admission fee of 2d was raised to 6d for the occasion.

The game justified its organiser's confidence in its public appeal by provoking a riot. The next morning the *London Magazine* described what happened.

> The company broke in, so that it was impossible for the game to be played out, and some of them being very much frightened, and others hurt, it could not be finished till this morning (14 July) when at 9.00 they will start to finish the same, hoping that the company will be so kind as to indulge them in not walking within the ring, which will not only be a great pleasure to them, but a general satisfaction to the whole.

The report does not mention the umpires or the reason for the riot. It was common practice for spectators to walk all over the field of play, though some important grounds, including the Artillery Ground, were beginning to put up boundary ropes to keep them out. The fact

37

that the London Magazine thought it worth appealing for good behaviour means that it reckoned the people behind the riot were literate and affluent enough to buy the magazine and read it.

The Artillery Ground was the setting for all the London Club's games and also the games of any London and Surrey clubs with enough money to hire it. The mid-eighteenth century was a golden age for Surrey cricket. Clubs sprang up all over the place. Among the greats were Mitcham, with its famous green, the scene of many an epic struggle and umpiring nightmare; Addington, which reckoned itself the best club in England in the 1740s, and Moulsey, many of whose players were Londoners.

London cricketers moved from club to club in and around London the same way country cricketers moved from patron to patron, and clubs like Moulsey which were near London had a thriving commerce in talented players. London cricket sponsors were a mixed bag: gentlemen, businessmen, cricket enthusiasts, arrivistes keen to strike a cricketing image, neighbourhood patriots. There were some aristocratic patrons of London cricket, but they had to be willing to operate in mixed company. By far the most influential was the Prince of Wales, who played and patronised cricket happily in any company.

On 6 July 1744 he commissioned a game between a London and Kent team and a Surrey and Sussex team. It was bound to be a success, with the Prince of Wales present and town and country feelings rampant. It was played at Moulsey Hurst, one of Surrey's best grounds. There was a huge crowd, of all classes, with a good number of women and hordes of Surrey loyalists keen to see London beaten. There was the usual multitude of boys and dogs wandering around. Dogs were a major hazard of early cricket, if anything more so in the town than the country; they wandered off the streets and out of the butchers' shops to piddle on the pitch and play with the ball.

At the end of the first day the game was unfinished

and the Prince and his noble friends ordered that it be finished the next day at the Artillery Ground. A London newspaper sent a reporter along but evidently he was not a cricket fan. He gave a tantalisingly incomplete summary of the first day's play – one side was thirty-one ahead with two of their second innings wickets down. The rest is a mystery. There was, of course, no mention of the umpires.

The umpire of a good London team or a good suburban team like Moulsey was often the team reserve and travelled the circuit of clubs and outlying villages with the team. There was not the direct personal dependence on the patron that often characterised country house cricket, but there was the same confusion of job and financial dependence, team loyalty and credibility as an arbiter.

In June 1735 there was a 'great match' at Moulsey Hurst between 'Surrey and some other countrymen' and a team of Londoners. The Londoners' best bowler, Ellis, dislocated his finger while throwing the ball about before the game began, had it pushed back in its socket and stood as umpire instead of playing. After the first hands (innings) London was seven runs ahead and the odds on them were 2/1. Ellis was allowed to play in the second hands but was soon out; the Londoners won easily without him. We don't know whether the man who replaced him as umpire when he went in to bat was one of the London team or one of its entourage. Probably it was the reserve who had substituted for him when he hurt his finger.

Reserves were in and out of the playing sides; sometimes they umpired, sometimes they played. This was an unstable situation and one which made the umpires nervous. As cricket steadily increased its popularity, the game began to look more like a feasible full-time job during the playing season, but only for players, not umpires. By the 1760s some players had short-term contracts for paid play, but these made no provision for the non-playing season and left their players as susceptible as ever to the bribes of bookies and gamblers.

London clubs were among the first to hire players for money. They had neither the means nor the wish to hire them by offering permanent accommodation and work, in the manner of the Duke of Richmond and other country house patrons.

There were only a few professional cricketers by mid-century, and no professional umpires. No-one wanted professional umpires. Team managers had better things to do with their money, and in fact sometimes did the umpiring themselves. A club's ideal was a handful of reliable umpires who could be stood down after a bad game but were glad to oblige when asked. It was becoming customary to give umpires a share of the winners' prize, though sometimes this was only given to the umpire of the winning side. In 1771 a Reading paper advertised 'a game of cricket for 11 good hats of 5/-value to be played on Tunworth Down on Whit Monday . . . A hat will be given to the umpire on the winning side . . .'

Umpires were obvious targets for bribes, but had to be careful to keep their image respectable enough to get a chance of standing again. A blatantly corrupt umpire, like an obviously incompetent one, had no future in cricket. Apart from the demands made by patrons, managers and players for something resembling a fair game, there was always the crowd, who rejoiced in showing what they thought of really bad umpires.

The middle of the century saw the emergence of more knowledgeable umpires more closely and steadily attached to the teams for which they worked. This was partly because by that time it was common for umpires to be retired players. Thomas Waymark is a good example. He played for a number of teams on the country house circuit in the eighteenth century, including the Duke of Richmond's. His health began to fail in the 1730s and he moved to Berkshire, where he worked for a miller and played cricket when he felt well enough. Waymark's career demonstrates the constant financial worries facing cricketers and the means they adopted to try and solve them.

In 1743 he played for Berks, Bucks and Middlesex

Some Umpiring Signals for this Australian Summer

against London and in 1744 he was in a side representing England against Kent, in which he dropped a crucial catch with the result that Kent won by one wicket. After disappearing from the records for five years, he turned up again in 1749, as umpire of a game at Halnaker between one of the Duke of Richmond's teams, which included the Duke's sons, and a team of local boys. A match report said simply that 'the umpire was Thomas Waymark, whom the Duke formerly kept to play cricket'.

Others made the same move from playing to umpiring, picking up other jobs where they could. Any well-established cricket circuit which knew the player concerned was a good hunting-ground for work, but a lot of player-umpires ended up in London or the suburbs, where there was a plentiful supply of clubs and the chance of a wider variety of jobs for the non-cricket season. The player-umpire transition became standard for good players and by the end of the century had helped to make umpiring something close to a serious job, not just a necessary evil taken on by anyone who was desperate enough.

That is not to say that all late eighteenth-century umpires were professionals. Hardly any of them were. Nevertheless, in the top ranks of cricket the job was taken more seriously as the game took itself more seriously. The first cricket laws, published in 1744 and revised in 1755, gave umpires a section to themselves, replete with duties and responsibilities.

The 1744 laws were 'settled by the Cricket Club (London Club) and played at the Artillery Ground, London', a measure of the central position of the club in London cricket and of London cricket in English cricket. The laws were the work of the club's president, the Prince of Wales, and its committee of 'noblemen and gentlemen of Kent, Surrey, Sussex, Middlesex and London'. It was a line-up with enough prestige to give its laws authority. They spread into general use; many of the laws were already standard but now everyone wanted them written and official. Eleven years later, in 1755, the laws were re-issued, with some minor alterations, by 'the several clubs, particularly that of the Star and Garter in Pall Mall', under the simple and stately title 'The Game of Cricket'.

The Star and Garter was a cricket club and pub. It is a sign of the continuing importance of pubs to cricket, in town and country alike, that it was in a pub that the laws of cricket were settled and published. Cricket was now an institution and pubs were its public head-quarters. A number of clubs met at the Star and Garter, which soon afterwards merged with the White Conduit Club in Islington to form the MCC.

The Star and Garter landlord was one of many publicans who were cricket club advisers, caretakers and groundsmen. He charged gate money to the pub's ground and in return issued tickets, cut the grass and put up boundary ropes or fences. He sold bats, balls and stumps. There was a thriving cottage industry making cricket balls in Kent in the 1760s, and the Star and Garter was one of its best customers. Team, club and general cricket notices were pinned up in the pub, which was the team's meeting-place before and after games. Cricket discussions kept the bar open half the night, while the landlord sold beer to his cricketing customers and brewed supplies for the next game. He advertised the Star and Garter games in the press and acted, like all cricketing publicans, as the club's front man, a public relations officer with an inside view of the game.

He did the club proud with the 1755 edition of the laws. They were printed in booklet form, with flourishes decorating the front page and big, ornate letters marking the start of each new section. The most noticeable quality of both sets of laws is how fundamentally similar they are to today's laws; the main difference is that there are far fewer of them. The laws of cricket and the duties of umpires have expanded steadily since the start of the game and have not yet shown any sign of stopping.

By 1755 umpires were more than primitive peace-keepers. Each umpire had jurisdiction over one end and now they were set up as authorities over it; their pronouncements were given an air of authority. Instead

43

of threatening players who disputed the umpire's decisions with being 'turned out and voided in the match', as recommended in the 1727 rules, the 1755 laws simply said that an umpire was to no-ball any bowler over-stepping the crease – 'and no person shall have any right to question him'.

The umpires' partners in their new-found glory were the scorers, whose duties had also expanded. In 1744 a score-card appeared for the first time, though most scorers still notched up the score on sticks. A Kent scorer recorded all the individual scores in a Kent/England game, all the byes, which meant all the extras – mainly overthrows, and gave the names of a catcher and stumper as well as a bowler. It was thirty years before such a detailed card was seen again.

The growing interest in cricket and the ever increasing betting on it created a demand for details of individual scores. There were bets on everything: how many runs a batsman would score, how he would be out, when, to whose bowling, at which end. By 1773 the best score-cards recorded how all the wickets were taken, not just the ones that were bowled and caught, with the occasional run-out. Scorers at sophisticated games kitted themselves out in smart clothes, moved out of the field of play and sat at tables, watching for umpires' signals and writing the score. Most cricket was pretty rough, and so were its notchers, but by 1775 scorers were second only to umpires as status symbols at clubs like the Star and Garter.

Umpires earned their status. The 1755 laws spelt out their growing burden of duties. There was a section called laws for strikers, which was all about how to be out, and made clear, if not simple, demands on umpires. There were the traditional ways of being out: hit wicket, stumped, handled the ball, hit the ball twice, and also a way which limited the earlier collision licence granted to batsmen: obstructing by running off the pitch to prevent a catch or run out.

There was one set of ways that a batsman could get himself out which makes no sense at all to a modern reader but was familiar to cricketers until the 1830s: nipped out. A nip was a little stroke, an accidental touch which was distinguished from a proper stroke but could get batsmen out in the same way as strokes, by being caught, hitting the ball twice or playing on. Mr Jenner-Fust remembered his cricketing days at Eton featuring a fielding position known as 'nips', or point, right up until 1823, when it changed its name to point. It was more like mid-off than the modern point position, and it was commonly assigned to good fielders who could hold a catch which a batsman spooned or nipped up to the off. Umpires disliked nips and preferred a stroke which was clearly and cleanly hit, but gave 'nipped himself out' decisions until the early nineteenth century.

There was no LBW in early cricket. A batsman with a long, curved bat was unlikely to stand in front of the wicket; he stood to the side and used his bat like a hockey stick. But the 1744 laws had sounded what may possibly have been the first warning shot against LBW in the form of a prohibition of 'standing unfair to strike'. That probably meant standing out of one's crease to receive the ball, so shortening the length of a run, but it could have meant standing in front of the wicket, so guarding it. The duty of stopping this unfair tactic had been assigned to the umpire. The 1755 laws made no mention of LBW. Leg play was still a rare abomination that was ignored with aplomb by umpires.

The next section dealt with a difficult issue: obstruction of the batsman. Obstruction was a much more common offence then than it is now. It was the obvious desperation tactic of a fielder in dire straits and this was the first attempt to put a stop to it, giving the umpire permission, in a compulsory sort of way, to order an incomplete, obstructed run to be notched up. The non-striker, however, could help prevent a catch by getting in the bowler's way anywhere within a bat's reach. Lucky umpire, measuring that one. Furthermore, the batsman could hit the ball twice if it was on the point of hitting his wicket. Dead ball was defined.

Umpires were to make sure that wicket-keepers stood

at 'a reasonable distance behind the wicket' and did not put the striker off. A cheerful piece of reliance on umpires' judgement and courage.

The section on umpires completed the process of dignifying, or at least expanding, their position. It covered all the basic umpiring tasks that had long since been accepted by all cricketers, but added the declaration that umpires were 'sole judges of all fair or unfair play'. Nevertheless umpires could still be changed during a game if both sides or patrons so desired. The balance of power was tipping in the umpires' favour but they could still not function with complete freedom.

Whether the new, fair, authoritative umpire, armed with knowledge of the laws, existed on the field as well as on paper is impossible to say. The little evidence there is all comes from big clubs and gives no idea of the state of umpiring in humble games. One especially nice report is about a game played on Walworth Common, Surrey, between Squire Hartley's XI and Squire Tatum's XI; the praise it pours on the umpire suggests as much that his umpiring was unusual as that it was excellent.

> The umpire was Mr William Austen, of the Lady and Cat in Barnaby St., who gave his judgement with the utmost impartiality, and received the thanks of the whole body, who afterwards had an elegant entertainment at his house.

London clubs had the same sense of local identity and pride as country clubs. London cricket was a conglomeration of village and club cricket, with a collective identity to lean on when the occasion arose. In matches between London clubs, local loyalty was predominant, but in any other matches London loyalty was predominant. Clubs like Walworth and Mitcham, although very close to London, had no doubt that they were Surrey clubs and relished nothing more than beating London at its own game. One of the biggest events of 1730 in Mitcham was the game between Mitcham and the 'Gentlemen of London', played on the club's famous green and umpired for Mitcham by one of its old cricket stars. But

Mitcham men became Londoners at once when there was a match against the provinces.

By the 1760s the most famous London club was the White Conduit Club, which took over the leadership of London cricket from the Star and Garter. It was not officially formed as a cricket club until 1790, but was functioning from the 1740s, if not before. White Conduit House, Islington, was built in 1735 and the cricket was played on White Conduit Fields. It profited from the popularity of White Conduit Gardens in the 1750s and became the most socially distinguished club in London.

But the game was not all wine and roses. There were plenty of people who disapproved of cricket and took particular exception to distinguished clubs which should have known better leading the country to ruin. In September 1743 the *Gentleman's Magazine* launched a furious attack against cricket, and incidentally gave a good picture of London cricket as a game for all classes, poisoned by that favourite evil of puritanical reformers – gambling.

> The time of people of fashion may be, indeed, of little value, but in a trading country, the time of the meanest man ought to be of some worth to himself and to the community . . . It draws numbers of people away from their employment to the ruin of their families . . . It is a most notorious breach of the laws, as it gives the most open encouragement to gaming, the advertisements most impudently reciting that great sums are laid . . .

Bookies followed the same circuit as clubs, especially clubs with a prosperous membership, offering odds and bribes. In June 1736 two famous Richmond players who had never been beaten played a single-wicket game against a couple of Londoners: Mr Wakeland, a distiller, and Mr George Oldner, occupation unrecorded. They had beaten the Londoners once before in a close game and the match attracted a lot of attention and a small army of London bookies.

A breast high ball hit one of the Richmond pair on the nose and broke it, bruising his face and blacking his eye in the process. He bled copiously, but 'some human

47

brutes who had laid against the Richmond men insisted that he should play on (the Londoners being then ahead) or lose the match'. The poor Richmond man was encrusted in bandages, his nose was cracked back into place, or as near to the right place as they could get it, and he staggered out to go on playing. But before he had faced a single ball his nose bled so badly he had to throw up his bat and, after fearful arguments and recriminations, it was agreed that the match should be re-played in two weeks.

That was the kind of fracas London umpires had to supervise. They played a formative part in eighteenth-century cricket and earned every penny, hat, pair of gloves, ordinary and pint of beer they were paid.

4

From Hambledon to London

'Every manoeuvre must be tried in a desperate state of
the game', wrote John Nyren in a little piece on match
management which he added to *The Cricketers Of My
Time*. Nyren is the romantic ideal of traditional cricket:
honest, brave (he fielded at silly point), conservative and
passionately loyal to his beloved Hampshire village of
Hambledon. He was also ruthless. He gave details of
some of the manoeuvres to be tried when losing a game,
such as putting on a fast bowler when there was a cloud
passing over to make it hard for the batsman to see.
Everything that was not illegal was fair. Indeed, it was
positively unsporting to give up without trying a few
good ploys.

Part of the appeal of cricket, especially rural cricket,
was that it was whole-hearted and had no time for culti-
vated notions of gentility. Except as last ditch law-givers,
it did not have much time for umpires. Among Nyren's
tricks to be tried *in extremis* were some hints about
pitching wickets:

> If your bowling is all fast, and your opponents have a
> slow bowler, pitch your wickets in a cross wind, that
> you may in some degree destroy the effect of the slow
> bowling.

One of his very few mentions of umpires is in a foot-
note to this piece of counsel, when he noted that pitching
wickets was now the province of the umpires, but as that
was obviously not how they did things at Hambledon,
he ignored it and got on with explaining his own ideas
about wicket pitching.

Umpiring was probably even harder in the country

49

than it was in the town. Country cricket was staunchly attached to old habits, such as ignoring umpires, and to local peculiarities and customs. Village umpires operated in a small world and mistakes were not easily forgiven. There was a flurry of new and revised laws in the 1770s and 1780s, all of which left Hambledon and the multitude of undistinguished cricketing villages in blissful ignorance, or unconcern, alone with their village rules, their traditions and their bets.

Since Hambledon cricket has been written up so wonderfully well by Nyren, the most enjoyable way of looking at country cricket umpires in the 1760s, 1770s and 1780s, while the game was changing fast, is to look at his account and see what it implies – it scarcely says anything directly – about umpires and their job. His only direct statement about umpires is a simple, impossibly demanding one which would apply equally well and be equally unrealistic to any period of cricket: 'Umpires should be men of known competence to judge all points of the game, also of good repute for honesty of mind – free from prejudice and partiality.'

When Nyren published his book in 1833, he was looking back on the great days of Hambledon cricket, for they were long since over. The strongest cricketing counties – Surrey, Sussex and Kent – had been playing London teams years before Hambledon was founded. Its first recorded game was in 1756 and ten years later it entered its golden age, twenty years during which, Nyren wrote: 'No XI in England could have had any chance with these men; and I think they might have beaten any two and twenty.' In 1772 they did beat twenty-two of England at Moulsey Hurst.

But even then London was beginning to entice the best players away and by the 1790s it had won its rivalry with Hambledon. The last page in the club's minute book, dated 21 September 1796, has the bleak entry 'No gentlemen'. The club died on its feet.

In its days of glory the first thing evident about Hambledon cricket is that it attracted enormous crowds:
Half the county would be present, and all their hearts

50

with us . . . Oh! it was a stirring sight to witness the multitude forming a complete and dense circle round that noble green.

The Hambledon team was, in effect, the Hampshire county team and its prestige had a cumulative effect – people went to watch it play because it was so famous, and it was so famous because it played so well.

Like every team at the time, the Hambledonians travelled long distances to away games, taking an umpire with them. Richard Hayes, a Kentish yeoman and cricket fan, kept a diary which made casual note of the vast distances he covered for the sake of cricket. On 26 June 1776 he left home at 7.00 a.m. to go and see Hampshire (*i.e.* Hambledon) play All England (*i.e.* Kent and a few others) at Sevenoaks. They played one hand (innings) each and Hampshire won by 75.

> They beat us in guarding their wickets and in standing out (probably standing out of the crease to hit early, but possibly deep fielding) too. They talk of having three stumps.

In fact a new version of the laws, brought out by a committee from Surrey, Sussex, Middlesex, Hampshire and London in 1774, had legalised a third stump, still with only one bail. A third stump was already in common, if erratic, use, but evidently they still played with two stumps at Sevenoaks. The Willett pottery collection at Brighton museum has a Staffordshire cream-ware jug showing a Kent *v* Middlesex match at the new Lord's ground in 1793, with two stump wickets. That may reflect the conservatism of the designer or a late survival of two stump wickets in sophisticated cricket.

Nyren said he thought Hambledon had changed to using three stumps in about 1779 or 1980, after a game in which 'Lumpy' Stevens had bowled clean through John Small's stumps three times without hitting them. It was one of the few changes of which Nyren approved. Not as much as the umpires must have approved. Life was considerably easier for them free of the nervous tension generated by the ball going between the stumps and leaving them unscathed.

In 1777, the year after Richard Hayes's report of the Sevenoaks match, the Kentish Gazette advertised another match there between the same teams for £1,000: 'The wicket to be pitched at 10.00 and to be played with three stumps, to shorten the game.' The game needed shortening because for the last ten years the balance between bat and ball had been evening out and by the late 1770s many village and county games were unresolved after two or three days, demanding an excessive stretch of concentration from players and umpires.

At first, according to Nyren, bowling sharpened its advantage.

> Then the practice of bowling length balls was introduced, which gave the bowler so great an advantage in the game, it became absolutely necessary to change the form of the bat, in order that the striker might be able to keep pace with the improvements.

Daisy-cutting bowling disappeared for ever and length, or bouncing, bowling replaced it, fast and rising like that of David Harris or low and twisting like that of Lamborn, 'The Little Farmer'. Slow, lob bowling to a length followed soon afterwards. The slow left-arm deliveries of Richard Nyren, the writer's father, were the first of a new fashion of bowling and so perplexed batsmen that he is said to have bowled 170 of them once for only one run.

From 1778 on, David Harris began to inspire Nyren to ecstasies with his graceful and insidious manner of bowling. He twisted the ball as he released it and sent down fast deliveries which rose after touching the ground, curling so that they often trapped the batsmens' fingers against their bats. 'To Harris's fine bowling, I attribute the great achievement that was made in hitting and above all in stopping', wrote Nyren. Forward play was the inevitable response to the new and more sophisticated bowling. Cricket had left its youth behind. Batsmen got used to blocking and found it much easier to block and cut length bowling with straight bats.

John Small of Hambledon was one of a number of batsmen who changed from a crooked to a straight bat so he could play his favourite stroke, the draw, better. The draw was a sort of extended sweep, right round, ending up with the ball being played between leg and wicket or under the leg. With a thin, curved bat it was almost impossible; a straight bat was the obvious answer. By the mid 1780s most cricketers had abandoned the old style of bat and taken to playing forward with straight bats.

Bowling and batting both went from strength to strength. Tom Boxall bowled for Hambledon from 1777 to 81, moving the ball from leg to off, to the consternation of batsmen. David Harris bowled fast rising balls which moved from off to leg. The Hambledon coach, Harry Hall, one of the original corpus of local Hambledonians, a gingerbread maker from Farnham, encouraged his batsmen to play forward, left elbow up, despite the force of conservative habit. Nyren approved of defensive forward play but had his doubts about the way the new style might develop.

> Sueter was the first player that I remember to have broken through the old rule of standing firm at the popping-crease for a length-ball. . . . I have indeed seen others (and the finest players too) go in, and hit the ball away; but I have also seen them out by doing so; the movement, therefore, at the best is a hazardous one.

It was a rough job, umpiring cricket in a period when it was working out risky developments. Nyren never mentioned umpires as being important in the process of putting new techniques into effect. It was not easy to change the rules of local games, any more than it was for umpires to enforce the changes.

Bats were limited to a maximum width of 4¼" by the Hambledon players, not the umpires. In a game against Reigate, Surrey, one of the Surrey and England batsmen, 'Shock' White, went out to the wicket with a bat as wide as the stumps, acting on the simple principle that if he kept the bat still in front of the stumps, he could not be bowled. He was forcibly held down by the Hambledon men, who declared on the spot that all future bats must be limited to 4¼″ width, and shaved down White's bat accordingly. This limit was confirmed by the 1774 laws.

Besides having to appease conservative resentment and the suspicion of opposition teams, umpires in country cricket had the continuing problem of keeping their patrons happy. Hambledon was a gentlemens' club and its less affluent players were liable to be lured away by talent spotting patrons. James Aylward, one of the original XI, was made Sir Horace Mann's bailiff immediately after he scored 167 for Hambledon against Kent in 1777.

The Duke of Dorset and Lord Tankerville played a few games for Hambledon and their interest in the club was constant and could sometimes be predatory. Even when they were just playing, not recruiting, their interest cost them a lot. On 8 July 1783 the Whitehall Evening Post quoted the Duke of Dorset's cricket expenses for a year as £1,000, excluding his really gargantuan expenditure on betting and entertainment. That was heavy pressure on an umpire, even if he owed his employment to the team, not directly to the Duke.

The Duke of Dorset was a muscle man about how cricket should be played. In 1778 the *Morning Post* gave a vivid account of his part in an England v Hampshire (Hambledon) match, in which the Duke was playing against, not for, Hambledon.

> The Hampshire people very impolitely swarmed round his bat so close as to impede his making a full stroke, his Grace gently expostulated with them on this unfair mode and pointed out their dangers, which having no effect, he, with proper spirit, made full play at a ball and in doing so brought one of the gentlemen to the ground.

Eighteenth-century crowds understood that sort of thing and the crowd backed off respectfully to a safer distance.

The last thing umpires wanted was a show of power from anyone influential in the team. The number of businessmen and influential local politicians who were taking to cricket was increasing, and middle class pressure on umpires, though sometimes subtler than when it came from aristocratic patrons, was widespread.

Usually, umpires were ex-players familiar with all the tricks they had tried themselves in their time, but still socially embarrassed by the decisions they had to make. The *Coventry Mercury* reported the 1789 Leicester/Coventry match, the return fixture following the 'scene of bloodshed' game the previous year, as a blatant piece of umpire-bullying and influence wielding: 'Clarke, who was declared out by both umpires the previous evening, made his appearance with his bat at the command of Mr Needham who exclaimed "Clarke, keep to your stumps: damn ye, Brown (the umpire), why do ye not call play?" . . . Needham swore that if Mr Bunbury, the Coventry umpire, would not let him go in again, the match should not be played out.'

It was not played out. It had to be abandoned. The umpires did outstandingly well to agree on their verdict and stick to it, even at the cost of the game, despite the fact that they came from opposing teams and faced such muscular bullying.

Nyren gave a marvellous description of the tension at a game between Hambledon and All England, where the pressure on the umpires was enormous, though exactly what form it took is unclear. Sir Horace Mann, mentioned in this extract, is reputed to have spent himself bust on cricket.

There was Sir Horace Mann, walking about, outside the ground, cutting down the daisies with his stick – a habit with him when he was agitated; the old farmers leaning forward upon their tall old staves, and the whole multitude perfectly still.'

Hambledon umpires, like most club umpires, were sometimes players who were slightly injured or could not play for some reason, or they might be club officials. It was a well-organised club with a committee, practices with fines for non-attendance, a host publican and a battery of sponsors and backers, including Sir Horace Mann. Umpires had the same burden of travelling as the players and were included in the arrangements the club made for players. Village teams frequently went the length of the county, if not further, to play a game. 'When a match was to be played at a distance, the whole XI, with the umpire and scorer, were conveyed in one caravan, built for their accommodation.'

Club games had the occasional aristocratic umpire, but they had their own problems to combat, and anyway only played now and again. Lord Winchilsea umpired a big game at Lords in 1787 and another in 1789, but this was unusual enough to be remarked upon.

In June 1768, when Hambledon was just starting to become famous, its officials expanded their activities beyond the village. The principal of the club umpired the third of a series of games between XI young women of Harting and XI women of Rogate, Sussex. Everyone agreed that in the first two matches the Harting women had acted 'as jockeys as well as cricketers', which I suppose means that they pushed, hit, kicked and jumped on their Rogate opposition, but they lost this game by 77 notches. The umpire was so delighted with it all that he offered Rogate the chance to play on the Hambledon ground, Broadhalfpenny Down, and have an ordinary in the Bat and Ball afterwards. They accepted.

It is rare to find an eighteenth-century umpire acting on his own initiative like that, and he would have been unlikely to do so had he not been the club principal. Even more rarely does an umpire put his feelings in writing, but on 9 July 1769 the umpire of a village game in Berkshire did a hatchet job in the *Reading Mercury* on one of the teams he had just been handling. The teams in question were Tilehurst and Burghfield and they scored 81 and 122 respectively in their first innings. Bad weather held up play – it must have been extremely bad if it held up an eighteenth-century match, when bowlers only ran up a few paces to bowl – and they decided to play the second innings the following Monday. But when Monday came Tilehurst refused to play or to pay the 2/ 6 each the players had staked on the game.

The umpire who wrote a report for the paper was the

Bowler. "How's THAT?"
Umpire. "WASN'T LOOKING. BUT IF 'E DOES IT AGAIN, 'E 'S OUT!"

Burghfield umpire, William Beadster, who probably had a bet on his team. He was livid when they failed to reach a result:
'This is therefore to give notice to all cricketers of unfair proceedings of the Tilehurst Party, and what every side may expect that shall engage to play a match against them.'

The 1774 code of laws acknowledged the pressure which gambling added to the game and included rules about it. The side or player with the most notches after two innings won the bets laid, unless it had been specified beforehand that only one innings counted. Under this ruling, Tilehurst would have had to play a second innings and would probably have lost.

Mr Beadster, however, was an exceptional umpire. In general, the less an umpire showed his feelings, the less vulnerable he was to trouble making. Unless of course the game was so light-hearted that even the umpire escaped attack. 'On Tuesday last, 9 June 1783, a match of cricket was played on Old Field, near Maidenhead, by eleven gentlemen by the name of Boult, all near relations, and the parish of Bray, which was decided in favour of the former, by a majority of 26 notches. The umpire and scorer were also named Boult, and nearly related to the eleven.' (*The London Magazine*)

Eighteenth-century cricket was fond of gimmicky and off-beat games, and fond of making its more prosaic games as decorative as possible. It was common for spectators who knew nothing about cricket to remark on what a colourful sight it was. By the 1780s, fashion conscious and sophisticated cricket teams were wearing white, often with embroidered badges or caps, or buttons engraved with the club's initials.

Smart clubs wore the traditional rig-out of leather shoes, silk breeches and white stockings. Hambledon was one of these. 'You would see a bump heave under the stocking and even the blood come through: I saw John Wells tear a finger-nail off against his shoe buckle in picking up a ball', said Billy Beldham, one of their star batsmen, in his memoirs.

Hambledon clung to their traditional colours and wore velvet caps, sky blue coats with black velvet collars and CC (cricket club) engraved on their buttons.

Umpires stood out from fielders mainly because they went on holding bat staves even when most clubs had long since given up the tapping of umpires' staves to score notches. By the 1780s these staves were quite often tucked under the arm, rather than held out in front. Umpires' colours and clothes, like those of players, varied locally, and tended to remain jauntier and more haphazard in the country than in London, but frock coats or some sort of dark over-jacket were common. Tall boots gave the best view of proceedings.

Umpires' duties began to grow. In 1787 *The Times* published a dry little piece put in, unusually, by the umpires of a game. It highlights the growing importance of umpires amid the strain and chaos of public reaction to cricket, and serves as a reminder of how much public reaction there was.

A few days ago, two Justices of the Peace sent their mandate to stop a game, which was playing for an evening's amusement, at cricket; but the messenger was desired to return with the players' humble service, and if they might depend upon justice being done them, they would be glad if the worthy Magistrate, for the sake of the peace, would do them the honour to be umpires.

In a period like the late eighteenth century when the game was developing fast, homespun cricket experts abounded, discoursing to umpires on the ins and outs of the new rules, the London game (the game according to the new rules), the rough game (the game according to local rules) and the club's traditions. Umpires who were on the receiving end, especially in areas ambitious for a sophisticated reputation, sometimes sighed for what Nyren called 'the remote and unfrequented villages of England, where the primitive manners, customs, and games of our ancestors survive in the perfection of rude and unadulterated simplicity.'

The simplicity was getting more adulterated all the time. Along with length and rising bowling, straight bats and new strokes, LBW entered umpires' lives to bring cricket's crude innocence to an end. Nyren's friend Tom Taylor was 'a most brilliant hitter, but his great fault lay in not sufficiently guarding his wicket.' He was often bowled while attempting the cut, the new, stylish stroke, because he could not resist cutting at straight balls. On one occasion he and another Hambledon batsman called Ring were what Beldham described as 'shabby' enough to protect their wickets with their feet. 'The bowlers found themselves defeated and the law was passed to make LBW out.'

The 1774 definition and prohibition of LBW was not a direct result of Tom Taylor's or Ring's action. It was becoming common practice to block with feet as well as bat. Accordingly, a batsman was to be given out if he 'puts his leg before the wicket with a design to stop the ball, and actually prevents the ball from hitting his wicket by it.'

LBW has been a thorn in umpires' sides and a psychological burden from that day to this. In Nyren's time, no-one knew which was more despicable – using your feet to guard your wicket or being given out LBW. It was the clause about intention which rankled and always led to the batsman accusing the umpire of either ignorance or slander. The next set of laws, brought out by the newly formed MCC in 1788, relieved the umpires of having to judge the batsman's intention by simply stating that he was out if he was hit by a ball which 'pitched in a straight line to the wicket, and would have hit it.'

Even so, it was not popular. It did not appear on any surviving scorecards until 1795, though this does not mean that umpires were abstaining from LBW convictions; rather that scorers were not distinguishing LBW dismissals from bowled out, any more than most of them distinguished stumped out, 'catched out' and run out from bowled out. The official LBW virgin was the Hon. J. Tufton who, batting for England against Surrey at Moulsey Hurst, LBW, bowled Wells in the first innings. There is no record of the umpire's name.

LBW is one of the decisions that can only be decided by the bowler's end umpire. In that respect, it stood out among the 1774 laws, which went a long way towards defusing suspicions that decisions went according to which umpire gave them by abolishing the absolute jurisdiction of each umpire over decisions at his end. It meant that umpires could consult each other on difficult decisions and ones where they were unsighted. One of the simplest causes of distrust was removed.

Oddly enough, one of the most common causes of trouble was 'catched out'. The 1774 laws do not mention umpires' jurisdiction over decisions about catches; it was taken for granted, and a permanent source of argument. There were furious altercations about whether fielders had caught balls with the help of their clothes, by knocking batsmen out of the way, or with hidden help from the ground. Good catchers were highly prized, especially in country cricket, where good clean catchers were umpires' favourites.

A report survives of one important match between Kent and Surrey in July 1762, for 100 guineas 'and thousands depending', which is a good indication of how easily 'catched out' decisions provoked arguments and how easily arguments could flare up into violence. Whether or not sloping ground was a contributory cause of this argument is not clear. This 'great match' was 'not decided' because of a dispute about a player 'catched out' in the first innings when Surrey were fifty ahead. The dispute quickly became a fight, with 'blows and broken heads and a challenge between two persons of distinction.'

There was so much 'confusion' that bets had to be withdrawn. It must have been very bad indeed if bookies agreed to refund bets.

Nyren rated all fielding highly. He described Hamble-don's best fielders darting all over the field like lightning and running swift as hares. Fielding was invaluable when playing on Windmill Down, to which the club moved when some of its players complained that the original ground, Broadhalfpenny Down, was too bleak. Windmill Down was, said Nyren, 'one of the finest places for playing on I ever saw', which means it had a flat pitch. But 'the ground gradually declined every way from the centre: the fieldsmen therefore were compelled to look about them, and for this reason they became so renowned in that department of the game.'

The umpires were unable to see what happened over the brow of the hill, even if they could confer. Trying to see over slopes such as Hambledon played on, and many far worse, was a routine problem for eighteenth-century umpires.

With matches commonly coming to an abrupt end because of disputes, a useful but dangerous tactic for umpires was to set a time limit for any team or player refusing to play, and if the game had not re-started when the time was up, the side refusing to play lost the game. From 1774 on, umpires only had to call play once, not three times, before awarding the match to the team that was willing to play. Even so, sides continued to walk off and sit down in protest with monotonous regularity. Usually they took their umpire with them but they might leave him behind if he proved unusually reluctant to support their action.

The overall impression given by the 1774 laws is one of keenness to improve umpires' relations – all relations: with each other, with players and with spectators. Troublesome matters such as deciding who should choose pitch and innings were eased off the umpires' shoulders. Visiting teams chose both, though if the game was played on a neutral ground, the leading bowlers tossed for innings. Still, London laws notwithstanding, it took a long time to change local customs on such issues.

It was not all easier going for umpires. They were expected to call short runs, which they had been doing for years unofficially. It was now an official, nerve-racking duty, and one local paper reported with evident relief and high spirits the foolishness of one of its umpires in calling a short run when the batsmen had only taken a single.

For the first time notches were called runs in the laws. The two names were about equally common at this time, notches being favoured by more traditional teams like Hambledon.

One of the simplest of the new laws was that, for the first time, the umpires could not be changed simply because both sides wanted them changed. In a way, this was a proclamation of umpires' independence from team and patronal pressure, like their emancipation from having their jurisdiction limited to one end. But how much notice country clubs took of this new rule is open to question, as is the difference, if any, it made to relations between players and umpires.

Nyren's book was purposely eulogistic: he gave a picture of the club he loved in its golden age, which had now passed it by, leaving it resplendent in his memory. Even so, the incidents he recounted do make it sound as if Hambledon matches, including important and tense ones, were cheerful.

> There was high feasting held on Broadhalfpenny during
> the solemnity of one of our grand matches. Oh! it was

a heart-stirring sight to witness the multitude forming a complete and dense circle round that noble green. Half the county would be present, and all their hearts with us – little Hambledon, pitted against All England was a proud thought for the Hampshire men. . . . How these fine brawn-faced fellows of farmers would drink to our success!

Nyren waxed lyrical on the ordinaries everyone consumed afterwards at the Bat and Ball. He was a musician and liked the singing as much as the ale and beef. 'Little George' Leer, Hambledon's best long-stop, used to celebrate the day's cricket in duet with Sueter, the wicket-keeper:

I have been there, and still would go,
'Twas like a little heaven below!

It would be nice, though probably unrealistic, to think that the Hambledon umpires went to these ordinaries and festivities.

Just a hint of the problems of umpiring, even at games as idyllic as Nyren described, can be found in his description of Sueter. Unlike Yalden, his opposite number in a team they often played, he did not 'shuffle and resort to trick.' Everyone respected him so much 'that I firmly believe they would have trusted to his decision, had he ever chosen to question that of the umpire.'

Every class, religion and temperament was represented at Hambledon and travelled together to and from matches and their accompanying celebrations. Umpires for away matches could hardly be excluded from these, unless they had disgraced themselves so badly that it was unsafe to be near the team. The Dukes of Dorset, Lennox and Albemarle and the Earl of Tankerville were among the team's members, who also included local landowners of varying degrees of prosperity, small businessmen, farmers, farm labourers and men from the country trades which always provided a lot of cricketers: blacksmiths, carpenters, horse dealers and trainers, wheelmakers and carters.

Nyren did not mention a Hambledon umpire by

name, nor did he say what class any of them were, though it is likely that for the most part they were rural tradesmen like the majority of the players. It is hard to imagine who would have put a country gentleman umpire under more strain – the Duke of Dorset or one of the Walker brothers, described by Nyren as 'hard, ungain, scrag-of-mutton frame; wilted, apple-john face . . . long spider legs, as thick at the ankles as at the hips . . . skin . . . like the rind of an old oak, and as sapless.'

Religion was no more divisive than class. One of the founders of Hambledon was Rev. Charles Powlett, third son of the Duke of Bolton, but Nyren was a Roman Catholic, in an age when being a Catholic was still deeply suspicious. His father, Richard Nyren, the captain and manager of the club, 'a good face-to-face, unflinching, uncompromising, independent man', was the grand-son of a Jacobite who had been condemned to death after the 1715 Jacobite uprising and reprieved; he was the son of a 1745 Jacobite. He held musical evenings at the Bat and Ball, as did his son the Hambledon chronicler, before going home to evening mass celebrated by French Jesuits. Class, faith and occupation were less important to eighteenth-century country cricketers and their umpires than skill and a durable temperament.

Nyren's account of Hambledon is wistfully, happily nostalgic, but tinged with sorrow and, intermittently, anger at the new styles of bowling that were evolving to worry lovers of tradition. Nyren died in 1837, by which time the new 'throwing-bowling' was firmly established in English cricket and the days of underarm pitching were slipping into the past. Nyren's book is a tribute to the first age of cricket. It is an epitaph for a style of cricket already in jeopardy, and it is fitting that Nyren should have touched on umpires only at moments of doubt and dissension. The perfect umpire in eighteenth-century cricket was the silent and self-effacing personification of power.

5

The Round-arm Controversy

The late eighteenth and early nineteenth centuries were when cricket became an institution. Thomas Lord established his famous ground on its first site in 1787, the year the Marylebone Cricket Club was founded. By the turn of the century the MCC was accepted everywhere as the official head-quarters of the game and Lord's as its home. Cricket developed a civil service, complete with a mass of rules and regulations, fixture lists, professional players, coaches and ground staff. The midlands and north emerged as playing areas to rival the south. In a period of expansion and development, the men who had the hardest time, were the umpires.

One awful exception to that was the umpire who came out of a clash at the Meadows Ground, Nottingham as the winner. In the early summer of 1811 he was umpiring a good humoured game when a young batsman called Thomas Tomms made a good stroke, ran three and in starting the fourth, ran straight into the umpire. Neither of them seemed badly hurt, Tomms went on playing but was out soon afterwards and obviously felt unwell. He lay down and died. It was an unusual effect for an umpire to have on a player.

Umpires usually produced effects, at best, of annoyance or impatience. Part policemen, part traffic-warden, they were doomed to unpopularity and went through half a century of trouble and grief. Although for the first time one or two of them did earn some respect from cricketers and the cricketing public, and by the 1830s there were character umpires as well known as famous players, most umpires were ignorant, incompetent, crude and partisan.

Nevertheless, there were some who were knowledgeable and neutral and a good number who were confident. They needed that confidence. The turn of the century saw an explosion of the controversy Nyren had been dreading, about round-arm bowling, until it dominated the game, leaving the MCC limping along in its wake, issuing impotent prohibitive laws. The burden of control fell upon umpires and for the most part they followed the legal principle that silence implies consent. It was a waste of time trying to resist the overwhelming pressure of round-arm bowling, which was transforming every level of cricket, and they left it alone.

The real question was how long it would be before the new law-giving authority, the MCC, legalised both the new style of bowling and the attitude taken towards it by most umpires. Between about 1780 and 1830, bowling brought into question the nature and true seat of authority in cricket. It was a horribly exciting time to be an umpire.

The MCC first came to public notice and to the brink of taking on its burden of official authority in June 1788, when a forthcoming match was advertised between Marylebone and the White Conduit Club. It was the

Point (appealing for catch at cricket). "" 'OW'S THAT?"
Umpire (supporter of batting side). "MIND YER OWN BUSINESS." (*Appeal dismissed.*)

White Conduit Club's last match and they lost it by 83 runs. In effect, the club had already been absorbed into the Marylebone Cricket Club, which instantly became the premier club in England.

One of its attendants when it was still the White Conduit Club was a Yorkshireman called Thomas Lord who worked at White Conduit House and ran a wine merchant's office in Gloucester Street, near Dorset Square. Lord, like Nyren, was from a Catholic, Jacobite family, but unlike Nyren he concealed, or abandoned, his faith when he came south. He built up his business, becoming wine supplier to the king and court, and used the profits to lease a square of land (the present Dorset Square) from the Portman family and the White Conduit Club. He leased this as a cricket ground to the Earl of Winchilsea, who was to become one of the leading lights of the MCC.

In 1808 he established a second and bigger ground at Lisson Grove, only to find it subject to a compulsory purchase order when the Regent's Canal was built in 1813. He moved his ground to its third home, in St John's Wood, where it still is today. By that time his cricket club was known by its initials, MCC, and its new ground became known as Lord's.

Even before the MCC had settled itself at Lord's, its reputation as the headquarters of English cricket was secure enough for it to publish a revised set of cricket laws, in May 1788. Their most noticeable feature is their lack of any reference to the new, advanced style of bowling, known as the 'march-of-intellect system', a term used to deride any radical and unwelcome plan of action such as the one for securing working class literacy. The MCC committee was traditionalist to the core and took the firm and altogether impracticable view that bowling must be underarm, without any jerking or raising of the arm to shoulder level for delivery, and it apparently went without saying that this was the rule the umpires had to enforce.

Umpires were in an impossible position. The gap between bowling law and practice had become too wide to be bridged. As early as 1780, Tom Walker of Hambledon had begun 'the system of throwing instead of bowling, now so much the fashion. At that time it was esteemed foul play, and so it was decided by a council of the Hambledon Club, which was called for the purpose' (Nyren). Hambledon was small enough to draw up club policy without too much trouble, though even they were to find its enforcement difficult. Hambledon players, like players everywhere, began bowling with the arm at shoulder level on delivery, a method known as round-arm for the simple reason that the arm came round with a sideways sweep at delivery, instead of coming up and under according to the old, underarm method so passionately supported by Nyren. He condemned round-arm bowling as 'throwing' and 'jerking', and applauded his club's stand against it.

Hambledon was so respected that its policy on anything to do with the game was taken as general, if unofficial, cricket policy. But by the turn of the century, Hambledon policy and official cricket policy notwithstanding, round-arm bowling was common everywhere. Its most famous early practitioner was John Willes, who became a leading campaigner for the new style. He is said to have realised how effective round-arm bowling could be when his sister bowled to him at home in the barn with her arm coming round high in the delivery swing, to avoid her crinolined skirts. He adopted her style of delivery, to devastating effect.

In July 1807 the *Sporting Magazine* reported a Kent *v* England match at Penenden Heath:

In this match the straight-arm (round-arm) bowling introduced by John Willes Esq. was generally practised and fully proved an obstacle in getting runs, in comparison to what might have been got by the straightforward bowling.

Bowling was keeping pace with the increasingly varied batting that was flourishing alongside it and had begun to dominate the game. There is no way of knowing how much round-arm bowling, also known as straight-arm bowling, there was by the turn of the century and how much of it was delivered not just with the arm straight but also even higher than the elbow, over-arm rather than round-arm.

Score-cards are no help because no-balls were not entered on score-cards until 1830, and even then straight-arm, bowling whether round-arm or over-arm, was not marked down under the no-balls. No-balls entered the laws, defined and re-defined, in 1811 and 1813, but the definition proved such a labour that both sets of laws were unworkable, umpires tactfully ignored them and straight-arm bowling went from strength to strength.

The essence of under-arm bowling was that it was delivered with the hand and lower part of the arm below the elbow. At least one or two under-arm bowlers with a high delivery, and therefore with dubious actions, were an embarrassment to the ruling body because they were, like the members of the ruling body, conservative. No-one could accuse them of being march-of-intellect radicals.

William Lambert was born in Surrey and was admired as probably the best all-rounder in the country. He was an attacking batsman in the modern style, playing forward to the pitch of the ball. He was a magnetic fielder and a slow, turning bowler. He bowled with his arm some distance out from his side, somewhere between round and under-arm. The embarrassing thing was that he was a believer in cricketing traditions and made it clear that, like Nyren, he thought round-arm bowling a fall from grace.

The MCC, the governing body of cricket, was unable to govern even its members, bowlers or umpires. These were objects of the greatest curiosity. When the MCC coach took its committee members to Nottingham in 1791 to watch cricket in the midlands and the north, where the game's popularity was growing daily, people crowded round to see Lords Winchilsea and Bentinck, Hon Col Lennox, Hon E. Bligh, Hon G. Monson, Captains Cumberland and Markham. People pointed at them in amazement. As for the committee, they were appalled by the 'jerking' and round-arm they saw, only equalled in iniquity by the tolerance umpires displayed towards such dangerous unorthodoxy.

Since by this time there were a good number of professional cricketers and most of them were bowlers, the situation was complicated still further. By 1835 the MCC had ten permanent professionals – five bowlers and five boys who were, as Thomas Lord had once been, a combination of ground-staff, fielders and general assistants. The rise of professionalism saw cricket divided by class. Amateur batsmen and professional bowlers became clear, though by no means fixed, categories: thus the throwing controversy was the obvious place for batting/bowling, amateur/professional, traditionalist/progressive tensions to be played out.

Inevitably, the MCC took the traditionalist line, on round-arm bowling as on the glories of amateur batting. It was something of a golden age for batting. The 1788 laws allowed, for the first time, the covering, mowing, rolling, watering and beating of the pitch during a match, with the consent of both sides. This improvement in conditions helped the development of new batting strokes, so that, to keep a balance between batting and bowling, the wickets were twice enlarged, up to their present size, but even then only the explosive arrival of round-arm bowling on the scene did anything to lessen the dominance of great batsmen like E. H. Budd, William Ward and Squire Osbaldeston.

In an attempt to contain batting scores within reasonable limits, boundary laws were passed in 1809. Six runs if the ball went out of the ground or over the crowd, four if it reached the boundary rope, and only three if the ball went into the crowd. This was to encourage more clubs to mark boundaries on their grounds. Boundaries were not common until the middle of the century, but their mention in the laws is testimony to the concern which the new dominance of batting was causing the MCC.

It was not batting which crowds went to see. No batting had anything like the effect on crowds that Willes

and his march-of-intellect bowling had. This report
came out in the *Morning Herald*, in 1821:

> Mr Willes and his bowling were frequently barred in
> making a match and he played sometimes amidst much
> uproar and confusion. Still he would persevere till the
> ring closed on the players, the stumps were lawlessly
> pulled up, and all came to a stand-still.

Umpires had no consistent policy on straight-arm and
round-arm bowling, and their varied rulings, with the
balance in favour of the march-of-intellect system,
removed any semblance of trust which players and spectators might have begun to place in them. In 1823 Mary
Russell Mitford published her article 'The Cricket
Match' in *The Lady's Magazine*. It is deservedly famous,
not just for its evocation of a village cricket match but
also of a village umpire and village feelings about him.

> A fourth imputed our defeat to the over civility of our
> umpire, George Gosseltine, a sleek, smooth, silky, soft-
> spoken person who stood with his little wand under his
> arm, smiling through all our disasters.

So notional was the idea of a neutral umpire, keen
only on justice, that one Midlands village club produced
this gem of a write-up on its umpire at the height of the
bowling controversy.

> Although in ordinary matches he gave general satisfac-
> tion, yet, taking into consideration the peculiarities of
> other umpires, he must be regarded as a little too fair
> for such important competitions as the Derbyshire and
> Wake Cups.

It was the players themselves, ignoring fair and unfair
umpires, MCC laws and opinions, who finally brought
about a resolution of the round-arm bowling question.
But only after the failure of a long official campaign.

The MCC organised a series of show-downs between
round-arm and under-arm bowling, hoping under-arm
would prove superior. Sussex, representing round-arm,
played three trial matches against England, representing
under-arm. Sussex won two and England one, though
the result of the last match was hotly disputed by Sussex.
In July 1822 another show-down was organised, between
Kent, with Willes opening the bowling, and the MCC

team. The MCC umpire was Henry Bentley, who no-balled every ball Willes bowled. Willes threw down the ball, stormed off the ground and rode away on his horse, seething with fury and swearing he would never play again.

Bentley had been a professional player and then an umpire for the MCC for over thirty years. He was one of the first umpires who was well known to the public. He lived in Lisson Grove, near the old Lord's Ground, played the flute and taught his two brothers cricket. One brother, John Bentley, was the groundsman of Vincent Square cricket ground and a champion hopper. He won twenty-nine hopping matches at Lord's, where cricket was only one of the activities, alongside hopping and foot-racing. In 1818 Bentley was finally beaten by a hopping doll-maker from Yorkshire.

Henry Bentley came from a family with a reputation for sporting ability. He was widely respected as a steady and teetotalling umpire, this last being an unusual quality worthy of note. When he left the MCC, the year of the Willes trouble, he went and worked as an umpire and coach first in Norwich, then in Somerset, until his death in 1836.

When he no-balled Willes, Bentley was obviously under great pressure from his club and ground-staff to do what the committee wanted. The most outspoken and influential MCC committee member at this time was Lord Frederick Beauclerk, great-grandson of Charles II and Nell Gwynn. He was an ill-tempered and charismatic figure who got a lot of mileage out of his outspoken support for the 'rigour of the game', by which he meant under-arm bowling and victory for the side he had backed. He claimed to make £600 a year out of betting. He rejoiced in being a brilliant slow, floating, under-arm amateur bowler and distinguished all-rounder, in being rude to players he disliked and in intimidating umpires like Bentley just by his presence.

When Willes left Lord's, never to play again, the leadership of the round-arm cause fell on two players who brought the issue to a climax and in so doing

72

'The Cricket Match', a painting attributed to Boitard and dated c1740-5: note the
position of the 'receiving' umpire close to the stumps

Cricket at Moulsey Hurst, from a picture attributed to Richard Wilson, R.A. The
umpires (with bats) evidently felt the spectators were not a problem to the players

Left: John Wilding, one of the first
'character' umpires

Below: J. Phillips, who did so much to
outlaw throwing

Kent v. Sussex at Brighton, 1849; from an engraving by W.H. Mason

Frank Chester, umpiring during the England–Australia Test at Nottingham, July 1948. In the first photograph he indicates 'one short'

Top: Syd Buller gives the West Indian
batsman B.F. Butcher out, ct. Parks
b. Titmus 44. The Test was at Old
Trafford, the first of the 1966 series.
Hunte is the other batsman. *Inset:*
Walking out with Frank Lee at the
Edgbaston Test of 1961

Right: The 'founder' of Bodyline, Douglas
Jardine, umpiring a village cricket match
after the war

revolutionised the game. William Lillywhite, 'The Nonpareil', was born on the Duke of Richmond's estate at Goodwood in 1792. He became a brickmaker then, following the cricketing tradition, landlord of a pub in Brighton. He never made much money from it because he played too much cricket. He got into money trouble and went up to London and joined the Lord's groundstaff.

In the mid 1820s, when he reached the peak of his career, the law still stated that balls had to be bowled with the hand and lower part of the arm below the elbow. Lillywhite was a bowler of variable pace, mostly slow, and bowled with his hand above his elbow. Officially, therefore, he was a thrower. He and a Sussex farmer Jem Broadbridge became the champions of round-arm bowling, ignoring, if not thriving on, official prohibitions.

When G. T. Knight, a gentleman and pillar of the MCC, adopted a high delivery style, higher than that of Lillywhite or Broadbridge, the MCC made him the subject of an official enquiry. The committee regarded him as an alarming example of the lengths to which straight arm bowling, once permitted, might stretch. The next stage after round-arm was over-arm, too grim to contemplate, and the next stage after an MCC member adopting it did not bear thinking about.

Undeterred by the MCC's condemnation, Knight argued his case in *The Sporting Magazine*, against conservatives who conjured up horrific visions which strike a familiar note with present day cricket fans – cricketers turned into armadillos, encased in armour plating to protect themselves from round-arm bowling. Knight pointed out that cricket in Kent and Sussex had happily allowed round-arm bowling for ten years and was armadillo-free. He went on to attack laws and umpires.

The whimsical caprice of umpires, arising from the faulty definition which now regulates the bowling, is so notorious to all cricketers as to need little illustration . . . at MCC itself the same bowler is allowed in one match and disallowed in another . . . everything is in the breast of the umpires; if he fancies you, he will let you bowl; if not, he will stop you.

There were innumerable examples to back up his argument. To take just one, in 1827 Nottingham and Sheffield played a provincial game of typical confusion and indecision on the Forest Ground, Nottingham. The chief Sheffield bowlers were no-balled several times, but not consistently, for unfair delivery. Play was suspended for several hours on the second day, the umpires were changed on the third day and the game was only finished because Major Taylor of the Sherwood Forest Cricket Club, one of the new umpires, talked Tom Marsden out of bowling with a high and jerking delivery.

Shortly after this the *Nottingham Review* reported that 'a letter was published asking spectators at Nottingham not to make offensive remarks to visitors. The practice of annoying opposing players has become too prevalent of late on the Nottinghamshire ground. Youths of 16 to 18 originated it from a friendly feeling to the Nottinghamshire players.' Their friendship was warmed by their support for Nottingham's round-arm bowlers and their impatience with visiting conservatives. They thought, as most people thought, that round-arm bowling was better than underarm bowling and that was all that mattered.

The fact that Lillywhite and Broadbridge were excellent bowlers helped the new law make its troubled way to the statute book. Their bowling was far too good to ignore. By the 1830s William Caldecourt had established himself as the first great character umpire and a powerful advisory force; he rated Lillywhite, quite simply, as the best bowler there had ever been. 'He bowled a hundred times better than any man did bowl: it was cruel to see how he would rattle about either the knuckles or the stumps.'

Successful round-arm bowling became a fact of life. Most round-armers bowled wides in great numbers, coming as they did from round the wicket with the bowling arm swinging round the body. Lillywhite, by contrast, used to 'dig them out', stumps and bails flying.

74

It made him the umpires' pet because it relieved them of the problem of wides.

Wides had become a plague. They were introduced into the laws in 1811, with a one run penalty attached, but were not written down by scorers as byes until 1828, when they were scored as wides, in immense numbers. In June 1836 Rev. Pycroft played a single wicket game with J. C. Ryle in which a total of 149 runs were scored, of which all 149 were untouched by the bat: 95 byes (round-arm bowling made life impossibly acrobatic for wicket-keepers), 44 wides and 10 no-balls.

In 1829 Lillywhite and Broadbridge bowled their accurate and unplayable best in a match at Lord's and were no-balled in the first innings and left alone in the second. After that, trying to stop round-arm bowling was like trying to turn back the tide. In July 1831 the *Bury and Norwich Post* reported that 'as throwing was tolerated at Lord's, the umpires (Bentley and Matthews) did not dare call 'no-ball' in the country.' In 1835 the MCC acknowledged the *fait accompli* and made round-arm bowling legal.

It was a great relief for umpires, who no longer had to enforce an impracticable law. Not that many of them had let that particular law inhibit them, but umpires were now taking laws in general more seriously. Cricket club committees were the nineteenth-century equivalent of eighteenth-century patrons, and powerful committees like that of the MCC could put the same sort of pressure on umpires. Henry Bentley is an example of a professional cricketer who, once he had become an umpire at Lord's, was placed in a position where his livelihood was at risk when he defied his employers' instructions to enforce their laws.

The humbler ranks of cricket left their umpires more room for personal and local interpretation of the laws, seasoned with local custom. Any robust village umpire would deplore servitude to the laws. The St Austell Club passed a resolution at the height of the Lillywhite trouble which spelt out its cheerful indifference, typical of most small country clubs, to MCC rules. Nothing showed this more clearly than the round-arm bowling controversy. 'Games should be played according to the rule of the Marylebone Club, but if the majority of the members wish to play the rough game, they may do so.'

6

'Character' Umpires

The long struggle about round-arm was an umpire's torment and led to the long struggle about over-arm bowling, which produced the first great character umpires. Any umpire with clear convictions about what was bowling and what was throwing and with the courage to proclaim his convictions on the cricket field was bound to be a star.

Most umpires were neither clear nor courageous about their views on over-arm bowling, which was universally practised by the 1840s. It is easy to see why. To take just one among a multitude of examples, the game between Darlington and Bishop Wearmouth on 10 August 1838 at Hendon, Sunderland 'ended abruptly because the Darlington bowlers began to throw and were no-balled by the Bishop Wearmouth umpire. Darlington refused to play on unless their throwing was allowed.' (*Sunderland Beacon*, 15 August 1838).

Many umpires resented the fact that dealing with the over-arm, like the round-arm, controversy, was made their responsibility. They reckoned the MCC or the leading teams should take action against illegal bowlers directly, then smaller clubs would follow suit and the problem would solve itself. Robert Thoms was a young umpire when the throwing controversy was reaching its peak in the 1850s and he favoured the invisible and persuasive umpire tactic. He talked privately to bowlers whose action he thought illegal, telling them it was they, not umpires, who must save the game by bowling with orthodox actions.

William Caldecourt was the commander-in-chief of

the opposite school of thought, the aggressive umpire brigade. He was born in 1802, the son of an esteemed umpire for Stockton-on-Tees and Lascelles Hall. He went to work as a ground boy at Lord's when he was nine and as a practice bowler when he was fifteen. From 1827 to 1840 he played for Hampshire and for the Players XI as a slashing batsman, good fielder and medium pace, underarm, practice bowler. He was an outstandingly successful coach at Harrow and Cambridge and, not surprisingly, a conservative about bowling. It is a sign of the times and of his stature as an umpire that it was when he became an umpire that he became famous.

At Lord's he was a great favourite, popular because he was conservative but at the same time very much his own man; he was the first to bat at Lord's in gloves – leather ones with wool padding – and he introduced his patent bowling machine, the catapulta, to the Lord's practice nets.

But it was as an umpire that he emerged as a phenomenon in his own right. The self-confident character umpire strode into cricket in the person of Caldecourt and made a heavy impression on the bowling controversy. He earned the nickname 'Honest Will Caldecourt' because he fearlessly no-balled all over-arm deliveries. In 1839, at a Sussex *v* MCC match at Lord's, he repeatedly no-balled Hodson, an over-arm bowler and the hero of Sussex. There was consternation, especially as Bartholemew Good, the umpire at the other end, did not call Hodson. The Sussex newspapers accused Caldecourt of partiality and launched a furious attack on him, which he doubtless enjoyed.

> Had Mr Caldecourt no regard for the opinions of Mr Good, his colleague? . . . the interference was ill-timed and manifested a hostile feeling to the Sussex players. Not one of the spectators approved of this decision, and it was repudiated by 9/10 of the gentlemen of the Marylebone Club – not the young players, but the veteran players, whose judgement Caldecourt, we are persuaded, will not be bold enough to question!

78

He was plenty bold enough. He and William Denison, the first famous cricket journalist, kept up a campaign against 'throwing bowling'. Questions were sent to Caldecourt to be settled as often as to the MCC. He went on no-balling, making the most of his reputation, or notoriety.

He stood close to the bowler's end wicket in a Napoleonic pose, wearing a tricorn hat, with one arm tucked into an enormous great-coat. The enclosed arm made frequent dramatic excursions to signal wides and no-balls. The law now let batsmen run as many as they liked for each wide, instead of scoring a fixed penalty of one, and wide signals made for some enterprising running. But it was the no-ball controversy which really set the game alight.

In 1845 the MCC began a final campaign against over-arm bowlers, starting with a new definition of a no-ball as any delivery with so dubious an action that it was 'difficult for the umpire at the bowler's wicket to judge whether the ball had been delivered with the true intent and meaning or not.' Umpires and professionals were forbidden to take part in games where obedience to the laws might be suspect. Caldecourt was in his element and earned his 'Honest Will' nickname and a torrent of abuse by no-balling everything he thought even remotely doubtful.

The campaign was fighting an uphill battle. Even if umpires were able to identify and call no-balls, they seldom did, especially not in the country. Henfield Cricket Club in Sussex recorded in its report of a single wicket match in 1845, in which a Mr Humphreys took 3 for 0,

> It must be observed that Mr Humphreys' bowling was not fair, being a kind of concealed throw. It was generally passed over and allowed in the country matches but it would never have been tolerated at Lord's.

That was an exalted view of the situation at Lord's. In 1851 every umpire was told. 'As it is impossible to define a throw or a jerk, he must form his own opinion.' After a further statement of this anarchic principle in

1858, the MCC gave in and made its first acknowledgement of the power of fact over theory in 1859 – it
instructed umpires to let the bowler's hand be raised as
high as the shoulder. Caldecourt spent more time at his
bat-making shop near Lord's, and less time umpiring.

In 1862 England played Surrey at the Oval in a match
shot through with north/south hostility. One of the
umpires was John Lillywhite, son of William Lillywhite
of round-arm fame, and he no-balled Willsher, the
leading Kent and England bowler, six times in a row
for bowling over-arm. The whole England team except
its two amateur members walked off and the 5,000 crowd
rushed on. The northerners in the England team were
convinced that calling the no-balls was a ploy by the
Surrey committee against the good, tough bowling which
northerners appreciated. Lillywhite was replaced by
another umpire and Willsher bowled untroubled for the
rest of the match.

This match was a turning-point. Until the England/
Surrey fixture was dropped in 1866, no England XI
playing in it was truly representative because northerners refused to play. The year after the disastrous 1862
match, the MCC asked county clubs their opinion of the
throwing/bowling question, got the reply that over-arm
should be allowed, and ignored it. Only in 1864 did the
MCC finally legalise over-arm bowling.

The 1864 volume of *Scores and Biographies* lamented:
This new rule would never have passed or found favour
with any having pretensions to the least knowledge of
the noble science, only it was found impossible to obtain
umpires (not only at Lord's, but all over the country)
who could, would, or 'dared' impartially carry out the
law as it existed previously.

The results for cricket of all this indecision were far-
reaching. It encouraged umpires to be doggedly self-
sufficient; there was no point looking to an ineffective
head-quarters for guidance. Even umpires with less
extrovert images made their names as individuals if they
were good. John Bayley of Surrey's famous Mitcham
Club, a breeches maker who was an MCC practice

80

bowler for thirty years, was much respected as a quiet and self-effacing umpire. For the first time, umpires began to appear by name in match notices and reports in the 1840s; people wanted to know who was umpiring a match so they could assess it properly.

Umpiring in the years of round-arm and over-arm bowling was, to take the most positive view, challenging. One of the many problems it produced for umpires was the virtual impossibility of judging LBW. In the round-arm years, an umpire standing about four yards back from the wicket, with the bowler delivering between him and the wicket, could not know whether the ball would have broken back and hit the stumps. Round-arm bowling was delivered from the extreme edge of the bowling-crease and nearly always swung across to the off, wide of the batsman, without breaking back.

In 1823 the LBW law was changed, requiring the ball to pitch in a straight line wicket to wicket. Nevertheless, some interesting, not to say enterprising, LBWs appeared in the records.

On 23 August 1826 in a match between Leighton Buzzard and Aylesbury one man, not satisfied with a conviction of leg before wicket, got himself out leg in wicket. LBW seems to have troubled amateur and small-time umpires as much then as it does now, though rather less frequently because, until batsmen started wearing pads in the 1880s, they naturally avoided playing the ball with their legs whenever possible. Still, LBW oddities were always cropping up. In a match between the Cambridge Union and Saffron Walden on 5 September 1826, one of the best Cambridge players, Sussums, 'was given out LBW by mistake in his second innings.' (*Cambridge Chronicle* 8 and 15 September).

Arm and hand before wicket featured in the scores recorded for provincial games, as did breast above wicket, and *Bell's Life* gave a terse little notice which summed up the state of early nineteenth-century LBW and umpiring. In a match between Rochdale and Denton on 26 September 1839 'John Dearman was given

81

out LBW to a ball which hit him on the shoulder, and the game ended in dispute.'

Even Dark, who owned the lease of Lord's and was in effect its owner, and Caldecourt, famous in his own right and famous in partnership with Dark as the best pair of umpires in the country, could not agree about LBW and in 1839 wrote to the MCC requesting a clear ruling. The ruling they received was a reversion to the 1788 law that the ball had to pitch 'in a straight line to the wicket' for an LBW dismissal, regardless of where it had been bowled from. Round-arm bowlers were still unlikely to get a wicket like that but over-arm bowlers, whose numbers were increasing daily, became habitual LBW appealers.

Some of the old-fashioned cricketers, like Alfred Mynn, the Lion of Kent in the 1830s and 1840s, thought it a mean way to get someone out and preferred to annihilate the stumps. But when Mynn did appeal for LBW, it took a brave umpire to refuse him, not just because of his eighteen stone bulk but because of the universal respect, bordering on reverence, in which players and umpires alike held him. Character umpires up against character players had no thornier battlefield than LBW.

One game which avoided this battlefield and 'created much diversion' (*Sporting Magazine*) was the Grand Veteran Match between one armed and one legged pensioners at Montpelier Gardens, Walworth. The first and second innings were played on 8 and 15 August, 'the weather being much to the disadvantage of the one legged players, who several times lost or broke their timbers, which disaster befell three of them on the last day.' Sadly, it looks from the scorecard as if the loss of timbers did not even out the odds by making the one legged team immune to LBW. 'As soon as the umpires declared the match to be in favour of the single arm cricketers, they drove off the ground in a triumphal car to Greenwich, with all the usual trophies of rejoicing and exultation.'

Conventional cricket had its fair share of players and

umpires who were contemptuous of LBW. Fuller Pilch was, like Mynn, a great Kentish player of the 1830s and 1840s; a great forward batsman, generally accepted as the best in the country; a bowler with an action somewhere between round-arm and over-arm who escaped being no-balled; the greatest single wicket player of the period and, when he retired from professional cricket in 1854, a professional umpire. He so despised LBW that anyone who appealed for it when he was umpiring got the gruff reply None o' that. Bowl 'em out. Bowl 'em out.'

The ultimate triumph for LBW as a force for chaos was the LBW decision which ended in a law case, Lane v Barnes, reported in *The Times* in dutifully matter-of-fact language in January 1853. James Lane and his brother John were batting for their local cricket club in a game against Westminster School. Christopher Barnes was bowling for the school. After getting drunk in the Wellington Tavern during a break for rain, he hit John Lane on the leg and appealed for LBW to the bowler's end umpire, who was his own brother and gave Lane 'out'. John Lane said he was not out.

> Further words of anger ensued, in the course of which the defendant (Barnes) struck the plaintiff (Lane) on the nose. This action induced the latter to dare its repetition, when the defendant seized a bat from his brother, the umpire, with which he attempted to strike the plaintiff . . . at length the plaintiff was brought down by a severe blow on the ankle. After this the persons upon the ground gathered round, and considerable irritation was manifested.

Lane spent weeks in bed with an infected and badly damaged ankle which cost him medical fees and lost him work he could ill afford; he was the chief assistant in his father's decorating and painting business. The court gave him £60 compensation. From our point of view, the interesting things about the case are the items the court noted in passing. The umpire, even at this comparatively late date, was holding a bat as a symbol of office; a break for rain meant a break for drink; the

83

crowd played its traditional, active role and the umpires played their traditional inactive but incendiary role, setting the argument off with a disputed decision.

This case centred round trying to change a player's mind. Usually it was the umpire's mind that had to be changed and usually less violent means were employed. The favourite instrument for persuasion of umpires was not violence, as in Lane *v* Barnes, but bribery. By the early nineteenth-century gambling on cricket had reached institutional status. Bookies had an allotted patch at Lord's, in front of the pavilion, where they took vast sums of money from players, spectators and umpires. Back in 1774, when cricket gambling was nearing its all-time peak, the *Chelmsford Chronicle* unleashed an attack on it.

'Cricket matches are now degenerated into business of importance.'

It cited stakes of up to £4,000 guineas on a single match and the selling of matches by players to bookies' 'legs'.

Umpires were not forbidden to bet until 1835, and the prohibition was extremely difficult to put into effect. Furthermore, even on the occasions when umpires were not betting, players and spectators gambled more than ever, free of the fear that their best efforts at 'fixing' might be foiled by an umpire with a fix of his own to look after.

Bookies' 'legs' were the principal 'fixers' and bribery agents. Billy Beldham of Hambledon recalled late in his life: 'These men would come down to The Green Man and Still and drink with us, and always said that those who backed us, or the 'nobs' as they called them, sold the matches.'

The Green Man and Still took over from the Star and Garter as the great cricketing pub in London and was the place where the intricate networks of bribery on big matches were worked out the night before the game. It was an expensive pub and young cricketers who stayed there because they were frightened of missing out on important information about umpires and bribes, frequently got into financial difficulties and were roped into selling the game by bookies' legs offering them quick money.

In 1837 Billy Beldham included in his reminiscences a few remarks about selling matches. Bets on games, he said, were often so high that it was worth punters' while to follow bets with bribes. Players often sold matches but not as often as people said. 'I will confess I once was sold myself by two men – one of whom could not bowl, and the other would not bat his bat – and lost £10. The next match, at Nottingham, I joined in selling, and got my money back.' It was the only time he let himself be bought 'and this was not for want of offers from C– and other turfmen . . .'

Later, when there were more professionals, and talented batsmen and bowlers were more evenly spread among clubs, it was harder to make sure of getting the desired outcome by bribing. In any case, all clubs, from the humblest to the most distinguished, grew steadily more conscious of their reputations and more anxious to provide play unpolluted by bribery.

It took a great scandal featuring a well known and well respected player to shake the cricket establishment into taking positive action against bribery. William Lambert, the great bowler and single wicket player of the 1810s, had an *annus mirabilis* in 1817 which included scoring the first pair of hundreds ever known to be scored in a match. At the end of his triumphant season he was accused of taking a bribe in return for not playing his best for England against Nottingham at Trent Bridge. Whether he did sell the match or not, enough influential punters were impoverished by the result and enough influential fans suspicious of his poor performance for him to be banned from ever playing again.

The next season, 1818, bookies were banned from Lord's and the on-the-spot selling of matches lessened. Away from Lord's, too, bribery lessened, helped by the decline in popularity of single wicket matches, which substantially lowered the amount of gambling. From the 1820s on, gambling on cricket began to decrease, though

85

in the 1820s and 1830s it was still heavy. In August 1834 the local paper at Twyford Down, Hampshire, reported that 'someone who had bet on Alton tried to bribe Richard Windebank, a Winchester player, to absent himself on the second day.'

Players often went absent from cricket matches, for a beer, a rest or whatever else appealed to them. Though umpires had the nastiest job in cricket, they do not seem to have taken themselves off as often as they were taken off against their wishes. But it did happen sometimes.

The cricket chronicle *Bell's Life* reported a match played on 12 August 1839 in Halifax between the Halifax Clarence Club and the Dalton Club. The report sounds hideously true to life. It rained non-stop. Halifax got 55, eight of their batsmen being stumped or run out on the slippery and uneven ground. Shoe spikes had been invented in 1800 but were not often used in provincial games like this one until mid-century.

Dalton lost two wickets and their third batsman was given out LBW. 'Play was stopped and the players left the ground in dispute. When play was resumed the Halifax umpire refused to officiate any longer and was replaced by a Dalton resident. Two more wickets fell, one bowled and one caught, and over the latter there was another dispute which brought an end to the match.' The only surprise is that umpires did not opt out more often.

In fact, the number of umpires in a game rose more often than it fell. It was quite common in the north to have four umpires, to avoid eccentric individual decisions, or two umpires and a referee to adjudicate on disputes between them. Not always successfully. On 7 August 1842 the *Hertfordshire County Press* reported a match between Hatfield and Ware in which Hatfield appealed to the referee against a decision by one of the umpires, a Mr Beecroft. The referee confirmed the Beecroft decision but Hatfield refused to continue. Sometimes there were even two referees, one for each side.

Some clubs still preferred gentleman umpires because they were thought to be less vulnerable to social and financial pressure. The only qualification laid down for anyone wanting to umpire the 1818 match between Nottinghamshire and England was that they should be gentlemen.

But there is no getting round the advice given to young cricketers by George Parr, the Lion of the North; it was perfect for dealing with the many new rich and minor gentry cutting themselves a figure in local life by umpiring local matches.

> When you play in a match, be sure not to forget to pay a little attention to the umpire. First of all enquire after his health, then say what a fine player his father was, and, finally, present him with a brace of birds or rabbits. This will give you confidence, and you will probably do well.

Any bit of extra income, any present, any gift, even if it verged on a bribe, was welcome. Umpires of important matches, such as county matches, were paid a pitifully small fee. A good number of county XIs were officially founded between 1839 and 1864 and circuits of inter-county competition organised. William Clarke's All Englanders, one of the great travelling teams so popular in the first half of the century, effectively started first class cricket in England in 1840 and county cricket flourished from then on.

But county umpires, like players, were only paid for six months of the year if they were lucky; usually they were paid match by match. Umpires of smaller matches generally got a share of the winnings, though at times that could be a Greek gift. Prizes in country matches in the 1820s, 30s and 40s included caps, gloves, gold rings, half crowns, ribbons, liquor, silver cups, waistcoats, wigs and, at a game played between two Berkshire XIs on 21 May 1827, two sheep and three lambs. How this prize was to be divided between winners and umpires was not specified.

With the rapid expansion of urban cricket in the early nineteenth century and the increase in the number of clubs all over the midlands and north, umpires were, as often as not, players who were having a game off, retired players or club officials and assistants. Only prosperous clubs kept on old players as paid umpires and these always rejoiced in reputations for knowing all the tricks.

Even so, serious games with serious umpires still produced umpire bullying. On 29 August 1829 Nottingham played Sheffield, and the *Sheffield Mercury* reported

> The umpires declared that they could not give him out, but several of the Nottingham players, headed by Denis, declared that they would leave the field if he did not go out. The umpires at length gave way to the clamours of the Nottingham players, and thus they had one whom they dreaded out of the way.

Nottingham won by 18. Their players and crowds were notoriously rough.

On 16 September 1837 the *Preston Chronicle* reported a match between Preston and Kirkham which featured umpires and referees for each side and a decision of 'called out LBW' for each side. The report mentioned in passing that one of the Preston batsmen, a superintendent of police called Mr Banister, saw the square leg umpire standing on the off side of the wicket, 'directly in the slip.'

While asking the umpire to move to the right side, Mr Banister was bowled. 'He was given not out by the umpire, but went out owing to the insistence of the Kirkham players.'

The standard of umpiring as a whole, though higher than it had been earlier, was still poor. In small games and local derbys it was primitive to a degree, but then so was the game it was handling and the forces weighing upon it. On 29 August 1833 Richmond played Reigate and the last man on the Richmond side was declared run out by the Reigate umpire. The batsman's brother was so indignant that he appealed to the crowd to seize the umpire and chuck him in the river. The umpire was only saved by the presence of a gang of his friends.

It was not always that bad. In 1814 the *York Herald* carried this delightful little notice:

> The Yarm players were extremely sorry that they had not had a favourable opportunity of returning thanks to

the umpires who had to go some distance after the game, and had their carriages waiting in the lane.

Umpires at village matches often had a simple and, as it were, innocently corrupt view of their job. Canon Robert Owen was an occasional player for Staffordshire and Derbyshire. After one match in the north with a particularly bad umpire, the canon asked him afterwards what he thought an umpire's duties were. This was his reply: 'Well, sir, I understand that when a property is to be disposed of each side appoints an umpire who does his best for his own side. So it is with cricket.'

One way in which umpires were always keen to proclaim their neutrality, however fictitious, was by wearing clothes which distinguished them from their team and so gave an impression of impartiality. In high class matches they continued to wear dark frock coats over breeches, while from the mid 1820s on, the players tended to wear trousers more often than breeches. If umpires wore hats, they might be beavers or tricorns. Many umpires still held a stick under the arm, usually a small one symbolic of authority, now that notches did not need to be tapped on it.

Village matches produced umpires and teams dressed in more varied uniforms. White was becoming the most popular colour but was still thought of as being 'uppish'; most country teams played in bright colours, wearing hats rather than caps. Alfred Mynn discarded his hat and took to a forage cap because of the danger of a 'hat fell on wicket' dismissal. In 1823 Brighton played Godalming and one of their players paid dearly for his fashionable hat when it fell off outside the crease. He bent over to recover it, lifted his back foot off the ground and was stumped. The penalty of 5 for fielding with the help of a hat remained.

By the 1840s coloured shirts, though still popular, began to give way to spotted or striped shirts and tall hats began to give way to bowler hats, at first only in working class clubs but, as time passed, more generally. Bowler hats, high-buttoned shirts and white trousers

89

became the standard uniform for almost all urban and professional cricketers.

By this time equipment was adapting to the faster bowling. Gloves had once been regarded with horror by cricket puritans, but were an inevitable addition to cricket kit with the introduction of round-arm bowling. Daniel Day patented tubular rubber gloves in 1827. Pads were the next addition. As Pycroft put it, 'It was not so much the speed of bowling, but the fly-about uncertainty of it . . . that gave rise to padding. Pads began to grow in size, shape and variety.' But they were not common until the 1880s, which must have pleased umpires, since unpadded legs discouraged batsmen from kicking the ball and precipitating contentious LBW appeals.

Only smart clubs covered their pitches, which were not rolled often, and hardly ever with a heavy roller. They were more loosely packed than modern pitches and drained more easily, especially as they were often on steeply sloping fields. *Scores and Biographies* provides this description of playing conditions in a game between Bradford Challengers and Dalton and Huddersfield in 1843. It gives an insight into some of the problems facing umpires:

> The Dalton and Huddersfield natives were a rough lot and treated the visitors shabbily. The ground was very rough except the bowling crease; the field was complete land and furrow.

That sort of surrounding was common. At Lord's the outfield was, literally, a field and was cropped by sheep which were penned in one corner. There were pony races between matches. The first lawnmowers appeared in 1830, but did not come into general use until the 1840s and not into general cricketing use until the 1850s. At that date Lord's still employed boys to pull the rough grass stalks out of the pitch before matches.

In 1859 Surrey refused to play at Lord's because the ground was so bad. But the Oval was nothing to write home about; it was used for executions in between games, with gallows pushed onto the field. Modern cricketers and umpires would consider nineteenth-century grounds unplayable, but it was rare for a game to be called off, or even postponed, because of the state of the ground or the weather.

Umpires were the judges of fair and unfair play but that was the nearest they got to decisions about when to come off or not to come off the field. In 1830 the umpires of a game between Biggleswade and Ware, Hertfordshire, were confronted with a Ware team determined to play on and a Biggleswade team refusing to play because of the bad weather. Powerless to decide or enforce a decision, they appealed to the MCC who said Biggleswade were in the right and awarded them the match.

Requests to the MCC for arbitration on difficult questions became more common, though for the most part local teams were cheerfully indifferent to laws and pronouncements issuing from London. Until 1854 substitutes were forbidden to bat, bowl, keep wicket or field in close positions, but this prohibition was widely ignored. In 1835 a law was passed that any side which was behind by 100 or more runs after the first innings must follow-on. Sometimes this was enforced, sometimes not. When follow-ons were enforced, it was often after negotiations between the captains and the umpires, regardless of the number of runs involved. Leg-byes were introduced into scores in 1848 but only appeared on score-cards when umpires felt like trying out their leg-bye signals, which was not often.

The traditional, inactive umpire was more common than the keen, modern umpire inebriated with MCC laws. Sometimes lazy or immobile umpires did their job sitting down. In 1840 William Ward, the great player, patron and restorer of Lord's, umpired that most energetic of propositions, a single-wicket match, between Hon Robert Grimston and a Mr Thesiger. To umpire it, he seated himself on a chair. In July 1882 there was a charity match at Nottingham which was deliberately in the old style: tall hats and spikeless shoes, no pads or gloves and 'the umpires, as of old, sat in cosy armchairs, smoking their long Broseleys'.

By modern standards nineteenth-century umpires were often decrepit. But then so were cricketers. Alfred Mynn's playing weight was eighteen stone. William Clarke was fifty-seven when he played his last game for Nottinghamshire. Fuller Pilch was fifty-one before he started umpiring at all, and stood puffing at his pipe before he gave decisions. He was healthy and performed confidently, if not always to popular taste. By contrast, the umpire of a game reported in the *Nottingham Review* on 8 July 1842 was portrayed with energetic contempt. 'If deafness and blindness were qualifications he excelled, but in all other particulars schoolboys would have been preferable.'

The general preference was for older umpires because they had more experience and because age gave them, *ipso facto*, authority over young players, some of whom were very young indeed. Tom Warsoys, the famous Nottinghamshire bowler, played an important game against the MCC in 1791 when he was only 12 or 13. Fitness and physical condition were less valued than toughness and determination, in players and umpires alike.

Ground facilities to support ageing umpires in their task were meagre. Their only strong point was alcohol. Hardly any grounds could provide lunch, though every ground in the country had a beer tent. In 1834 William Clarke challenged and beat at single wicket no fewer than eleven publicans who had put up drinking booths on the Nottingham ground.

From mid-century onwards facilities improved. Lord's installed the first telegraph scoring system in 1846, with the scores clearly visible on a board, and the Oval followed suit two years later. With the help of this, umpires could see at once how many of their signals were ignored or misinterpreted.

The press were ignored until 1867, so match reports were few, short and uninhibited, influenced mainly by the weather and the beer. In 1843 Tom Hunt beat XI of Knaresborough on three days' play. The local paper reported succinctly:

There was no play on 10th, although all the players were present. The Knaresborough umpire was intoxicated, and there was nobody else available.

Umpire to scorer became a regular job transition as the number of professional umpires increased. Caldecourt and Bayley became scorers at Lord's when they retired from umpiring. Pycroft saw them there one day and was saddened at the sight: they were sitting on kitchen chairs with a bottle of black ink tied to an old stump to keep it safe, 'an uncomfortable length of paper on their knees, and large tin telegraph letters above their heads. . . . 'Tis a pity two such men should EVER not be umpires.'

Retired umpires in the mid-nineteenth century were survivors of the most difficult and exciting age umpires had yet known. On the whole, umpires were more respected in 1860 than they had been fifty years before, but theirs was still a devil of a job.

7

The Age of Grace

Cricket became an international game in the second half of the nineteenth century. It also became a more organised game. By the 1880s first class cricket had developed a civil service and the ideal first class umpire was a sort of civil servant dogsbody – quiet, sober, knowledgeable and neutral. After the character umpire era came the quiet umpire era, overshadowed by the imperious personality and play of W. G. Grace.

But for the sparkle engendered by Grace and the outback Australians on tour in the 1870s, cricket might have fallen prey to dullness. It was shackled now with the official approval of the Church. The earliest known use of the expression 'it's not cricket' was in Rev. Pycroft's book *The Cricket Field*, 1851. Pycroft was not a dull man but the fact that he was ordained helped to give the game its claim to ethical behaviour which has been both its charm and a source of moral flatulence ever since. It is fitting that Pycroft should have coined the phrase 'it's not cricket' when criticising Grace. 'Why then, we will not say that anything that hardest of hitters and thorough cricketer does is not cricket, but certainly it's anything but play.'

Muscular Christianity instilled the Pycroft brand of good behaviour, which Grace despised, into public school boys by means of team games, and cricket in particular. Dean Farrar, the head of Marlborough College from 1871 to 1876, disliked sport but seized on cricket's virtues to fuel his sermons. '. . . to play out tenaciously to the very last a losing game, ready to accept defeat but trying to the end to turn it into victory.

Well, believe me, you want the very same good qualities in the great cricket field of life.'

Most mid-Victorian clergy were less high-flying about cricket. They overcame their objections to it as a hotbed of gambling and drinking because the gambling lessened and the drinking, though always impressive, was restricted by the introduction of licensing laws in 1872. Cricket was less objectionable than cock-fighting or bull-baiting. The vicar of Camber, Kent, gave his simple view of the matter in 1866: 'I established cricket not so much for my own amusement but because it improved the morals of the labouring classes and often kept them from places where they could come to harm.'

If ever there was a candidate for championing the Christian good behaviour principle in all its propriety, it was the Victorian umpire, as envisaged by idealists and moralists. But umpires, though they continued to take themselves more seriously and to improve themselves, never succeeded in making themselves conspicuously virtuous.

The cricket writer 'Quid' wrote an appreciation of umpires in 1866, a portrait of the ideal modified by experience:

An umpire should be a man – they are, for the most part, old women; and he should have a thorough initiation into the laws of the game . . . he should be able to count correctly, at least up to four [at that time the number of runs in an over] . . . He should avoid conversation with the field, should be above all suspicion of bias, and free from all odours of the tavern.

There was much discussion about the theory and image of umpiring in the second half of the century because contemporary thinking was no longer completely absorbed by the round-arm and over-arm controversies. Umpiring was a quieter job now, open to the intellectual exercises of cricket theorists. One reason umpires played a less assertive part in the game than Caldecourt and Pilch was that there was less need for them to. The twenty years after the round-arm and over-arm troubles were a period of calm.

But stability did not mean sweetness and light. The 1860s and 70s were a time of bitter rivalry and tension in cricket, with the first manifestations of widespread class trouble. North/south rivalry was extremely fierce. Umpires might have an easier time of it but the social background of cricket was showing signs of strain.

The connections between class and umpiring in Victorian cricket were difficult to deal with. All the accusations made against first class umpires at the time were of bias in favour of gentlemen and amateurs against players and professionals. In 1874 the Gentlemen won the annual Gentlemen *v* Players match by 60 runs. In his second innings for the Gentlemen W. G. Grace hit a ball back to Lilly, the bowler, which he would have caught if W. G. had not obstructed him. There was an appeal to both umpires, G. Keeble and A. Luff, for obstruction, which had been made an offence in 1864. The appeal was given not out, to the fury of the players. *Wisden*'s match report made the complaint which the Australians echoed on their tour four years later: 'Nearly every appeal by a gentleman was decided affirmatively,

"Private Johnson—About-turn!"

and the players' appeals were mainly met with NOT OUT!'

In this case it is hard to know whether it was the social superiority of amateur status or the cricketing superiority of W. G. which had most intimidated the umpires. If there *was* class bias in umpiring, it can be partly explained by the fact that, while most first class teams had only one or two amateur players, nearly all teams had amateur captains. And since first class umpires, retired professional players almost to a man, had an instinctive deference to the captains' wishes, knowing they played a large part in choosing the teams, there was an unmistakeable air of intrinsic virtue surrounding amateur captains, which umpires found inhibiting.

In some parts of the world, class figured in cricket even more blatantly. Cricket was introduced to the Fiji Islands in about 1870. Its typical setting was a clearing on a steep hill covered with coconut and orange trees, sloping down into the sea. According to the governors, the islanders were good throwing bowlers because they spent a lot of their time throwing oranges at each other. The chiefs took up the bat again as soon as they were out and umpires had the thankless task of explaining to them that the same rules applied to them as to everyone else.

Umpires carried bats as symbols of their authority and the more remote the islands the more they needed them. In the Lau Islands the opposition captain had to crawl to the chief on hands and knees to ask permission to change bowler, and the umpire had to contend with the chief's herald standing in the sea chanting the praises of every shot his master played, however pathetic.

English cricket's class troubles were tame by comparison. But when class was not a problem, there was always crowd trouble to keep umpires busy.

Nowhere was cricket more classless, rough and tough than Australia, right from its early nineteenth-century beginnings. When Lord Harris took an English team out there in 1879 the game at Sydney was disrupted when

97

the crowd invaded the pitch after a decision they disliked. They were a full-blooded lot. Lord Harris was attacked by one of them while protecting an umpire; mounted police had to rescue him and break up the mêlée. Nor was it only international matches that suffered; a player called Fairfax, of New South Wales, left cricket for ever because of the barracking he received in a state match.

Grace put his views on Australian affairs bluntly after coming back from tour there: 'Australia has always lacked good umpires.' He thought this one of the reasons crowd troubles so often erupted and so often had to be handled by the police.

Whether abroad or at home, crowds and players were always most troublesome about LBW decisions. *The Brechin Advertiser* reported a match between Brechin and Arbroath which demonstrated the impotence of local umpiring in the face of local anger about LBW and, possibly, bias against a professional player.

> When Arbroath had got the poor total of 21 for 5 wickets an unfortunate dispute arose. Lazenby, the Arbroath professional, was given out LBW before he had scored. After leaving the wicket he pitched his bat up in the air, and at once the umpire's decision was challenged by the Arbroath men. After a short altercation the Brechin club, with the view of getting the match played out, offered to allow Lazenby to resume his bat, but the Arbroath captain declined, and his team left the field, greatly to the disappointment of the crowd of spectators.

Spectators wanted to see their heroes batting, and no-one was more of a public hero than Grace. He was the umpires' biggest single problem, and not just in first class cricket. He inspired a whole generation of cricketers in every class of cricket to dream of dominating cricket as he did, overwhelming players and umpires alike.

Some first class umpires survived well and upheld the proud tradition of independence set by Caldecourt and other brave figures of the 'throwing bowling' era, 'Bob' Thoms umpired pretty well every major Middlesex match of the 1860s and was never accused of weakness or bias. His style of umpiring might have been subdued – he talked to the players and listened to their views – but he was never open to negotiation over his decisions. Devoted to the game, he used to clean the mud off the players' boots with a penknife, which he said was his most precious possession; money could not buy it.

The newly confident and conscientious county cricket circuit was becoming ambitious. It wanted its umpires' neutrality to be official. Until 1883 counties took their own umpires to matches, and with them inevitably the traditional problems of allegiance and fairness. Another of the characteristics of umpires from mid-century on was their close friendship with the players, who were, as often as not, their old team-mates. There were constant complaints about partiality and in 1883 the nine counties in the county championship agreed to change the system. Each of them sent the names of at least two umpires to the MCC secretary, who appointed two for each county match, making sure they were not from either of the counties playing.

Umpires like 'Bob' Thoms who maintained their independence and their friendships were greatly valued. People asked 'Bob' Thoms and Tom Barker, another favourite umpire, their opinion on difficult questions, often during play. They got as many queries and requests for advice as the MCC. In first class cricket the puppet umpire was a thing of the past.

Even in club cricket umpires' relations with players improved. On 22 and 23 September 1863 Deptford Unity played XI of England 'for the benefit of Charles Farr, umpire and bowler on the Deptford Ground'.

Still, one must resist looking at this period of cricket through rose-tinted spectacles. Good relations did not guarantee good behaviour. In 1866 'Quid' included this observation in his appreciation of the short leg fielding position: 'Don't let him talk to the umpire, but don't let him shrink from knocking that individual down, should it be necessary to do so in order to make a catch.'

In serious but not quite first class matches, rough treatment still made impartial umpires hard to come by.

David Rich played for Brechin Cricket Club for years, then retired and became its umpire. He was often chosen to umpire Angus county matches 'where neutral men were desired' because he was frank and untroubled about giving his decisions.

A thick skin was a great asset in umpiring. Any umpire in a game featuring Grace needed to be immune to embarrassment and, ideally, completely insensitive. Grace played his first big London game in 1855, with his two brothers, when he was sixteen. He never looked back. As he grew more famous with every passing year, he grew more certain that the crowds had come to watch him play, not to see him dismissed by an umpire ridiculously subservient to the laws. He claimed to be educating umpires, especially when playing with his brother, E. M. Grace, who had a similarly sturdy view of umpires' duties.

Stories about Grace telling umpires to shut up and let him get on with it are legion. But in a way he also simplified umpiring because he killed off fast bowling with all its accompanying problems for umpires of suspect throwing and foot dragging. Lawn mowers and W. G. Grace made the 1860s and 70s a golden age for batsmen and made the most difficult problems for umpires, batting problems: LBW, run out and obstructing the field. R. A. H. Mitchell, one of the great amateur batsmen of the 1870s, said he believed there were more such dismissals than before because pitches were better and fewer players were clean bowled by shooters or badly bouncing balls.

Closely mown pitches, rolled between innings, watered and covered to improve the grass, helped to produce a harvest of big scores in the Grace era. But improved first class pitches could still be nasty. In 1868 F. Gale wrote this appreciation of a wicket at Lord's on which Grace got 134 not out for the Gentlemen against the Players.

> The wicket reminded me of a middle-aged gentleman's head of hair when the middle-aged gentleman, to conceal the baldness of his crown, applies a pair of wet brushes

to some favourite long locks and brushes them across the top of his head. So with the wicket. The place where the ball pitched was covered with rough grass wetted and rolled down. It never had been, and never could be, good turf.

Humbler clubs never had any delusions about their turf. Cricket outside the first class circuit presented its usual variety of pitch types, ranging from the temperamental to the apocalyptic.

Bad pitch conditions were worsened by the summer of 1868, which was probably the hottest of the century. 'Heat stopped play' was a common entry on score-cards. Though capable of scandalous immobility, umpires were, nevertheless, the only men who had to be on the field all day and those belonging to smarter sides must have found 1868 atrociously hot because they were obliged to wear the white, knee-length coats, introduced in 1861, which made another unwelcome layer.

The white coats came on the scene during a game between a United All England XI and 16 Free Foresters, one of the many travelling amateur teams. The batsman complained he could not see the bowler's hand 'against the body of the umpire'. Someone lent the umpire a long white cotton jacket and soon afterwards these coats became a familiar sight in first class and, increasingly, in all cricket matches.

The weather, like accidents, is unpopular with umpires because it requires immediate action not catered for in the rules. Besides heat waves, Victorian cricket had its share of accidents which showed up the usual range of umpiring inability. One match at Uckfield, Sussex, in August 1884 brought together weather, accidents and umpiring which were, apparently, all eccentric. The batting side needed five runs to win with five wickets standing. The first of the five batsmen was bowled, the second stumped, the third run out, the fourth hit his wicket and the fifth fell down in the middle of the pitch without scoring a run. The batting side lost and the local paper commented 'the result was put down to the heat of the weather and the incompetence of the umpires.'

Accidents such as the batsman falling down were favourite bones of contention in village and local cricket; umpires usually did not know what to do and if they did know, they were ignored.

Accidents to umpires were more common then than they are nowadays, at least in part because of a general fondness for relaxation and beer before, during and after play. On 18, 19 and 20 September 1884 Umpire C. H. Ellis was unable to stand for his county in their match at Hove 'owing to a severe cut on his hand, received at Lewes while attending to the victualling department.'

Another reason for the number of injured umpires is that they stood much closer in at square leg than they do now, though less close in than they had done earlier. Records abound of umpires being hit by balls and giving the batsman out because it hurt. At Burley, Yorkshire, in 1870 the square leg umpire had his wooden leg snapped in half by a hard hit ball and had to be carried off and taken home in a cab. A few years later Tom Emmett, the redoubtable Yorkshireman, was nearly killed umpiring a match near Rugby. The batsman hit the ball straight at him, hard, because Emmett had sat on the pitch and shouted with laughter when asked for guard.

None of these tables was enough to slow the trend towards aggressive batting, of which Grace was the champion. He did not let the small change of injuries, county qualifications, previous engagements or eligibility problems stop him playing whenever and wherever he liked. He was forever giving exhibition matches and displaying his mastery of the bat and of umpires.

He became a figure of mythological importance. There are traces of Grace inspiration in accounts of umpire harrassment and over-riding of the rules in all sorts of matches throughout the 1870s and 1880s; if anything, more in humble matches, since smart players had learnt from experience to view his behaviour with slightly qualified admiration.

AUSTRALIANS v. THORNTIN'S XI at ORLEANS HOUSE, 1878
Spofthorth bowling to Walker

Grace did not need reasons for arguing with umpires. He just argued. Since 1845 it had been laid down that umpires should change ends between innings, which must have been a welcome development for them, indeed an unspeakably welcome one when Grace was playing. He was a great man for tricks which, while not strictly illegal, were less than fair, such as pointing to non-existent flocks of birds flying across a dazzling sun, then bowling while the batsman was still dazzled. Usually that sort of behaviour was more common in small club and village cricket, but Grace brought it into first class cricket without compunction.

One of the umpire's main enemies in those years, one which Grace worsened with his long innings but relieved with his tricks, was boredom. In response to batsmen's overall supremacy, sides put on endless supplies of accurate medium pace bowlers. In 1875 Alfred Shaw bowled 20 successive maidens for Nottinghamshire against MCC at Lord's. The following year he bowled 23 successive maidens for the North against the South at Nottingham.

It was only in the 1880s that off-breaks relieved the

tedium of defensive bowling. Medium pace attacks bowled to packed off-side fields and even the great man himself had to develop a half-forward, half-backward shot to avoid being caught there.

At Cheltenham once he was furious after getting himself caught off a boring delivery and put himself on to bowl, hit the batsman on the leg and appealed for LBW. The umpire hesitated and Grace strode down the pitch shouting 'Pavilion, you, sir,' The batsman went.

Although outright umpire bullying was becoming less common in first class cricket, except when Grace was playing, it still happened. Jimmy Dean, the famous mid-century player and umpire for Sussex, gave a decision which decided the outcome of the match. It provoked such anger among supporters of the beaten side that they set off after him, armed with a variety of makeshift weapons, until he pleaded sanctuary at Lord's through the Tavern window and was hauled in to safety.

At least there do not seem to have been the violent attacks on umpires, even when Grace was playing, which characterised Japanese cricket and made it a kind of samurai sport for umpires. The first recorded game in Japan was in 1863, between the British fleet and Yokohama, amid such unrest that the players were armed to the teeth and warmed up for their umpire assaults by beating each other up with wild screams when the mood took them.

English cricket, in its prosaic way, did usually have a reason for its conflicts, though this was often ignoble. An unexpectedly common cause of trouble was the miscounting of runs, especially in long innings. Some grounds had boundaries but it was more common for hits still to be run out. Miscounts were almost impossible to avoid when runs accumulated after the ball had been hit into the crowd or into long grass, trees, water or any of the other hazards surrounding old cricket grounds.

In July 1872 the Gentlemen of Shropshire were playing the Gentlemen of Hereford and just before close of play, 'Mr Wainwright hit a ball into the river, the umpire calling six for it. (Only hits out of the ground

104

Fashion at the Crease *Left:* David Constant, with square-leg companion Phillippe Edmunds, in crash helmet. *Below:* The well-dressed Australian umpire: Lillee bowls to Clive Lloyd during a one-day international at Sydney, 1980

Above: The West Indian approach: Umpire Gayle watches Patrick Patterson during the first Test of West Indies v. England, Jamaica 1986
Right: The women's game: Umpire J. Bragger concentrates as Sharon Tredrea of Australia bowls during the second Test against England, Edgbaston 1976

Above and left: The incident during the Edgbaston Test of 1973 when Rohan Kanhai objected to Arthur Fagg giving Geoffrey Boycott 'not out' to an appeal for a catch by wicketkeeper Deryck Murray off Keith Boyce. Fagg left the field in disgust, to return the following day and give a friendly pat to Kanhai during an over-change

The same year, different pressures: West Indian fans surround the umpires at The Oval after their team's victory in the final Test

The bomb scare at Lord's during the third Test in 1973. Dickie Bird and the West Indian players show their dismay

The opening Test at Edgbaston, in 1982: Pakistan supporters make their views plain

Last of the 'star' umpires? Dickie Bird in familiar pose during the fourth Test, England
v. Australia, at Old Trafford in 1985

scored six.) The captain disputed it being hit clean into the water, and allowed four for it, and all left the field, one more ball being wanted to complete the over.'

There were a surprising number of scoring disputes in urban club cricket too, where the situation was exacerbated by rough pitches. The Birmingham League came into existence in 1888 mainly because there were so many arguments about bad umpiring and faulty scoring among clubs in the Birmingham and District Cricket Association. The League system of appointing neutral umpires had its roots in the chaos produced by bad umpires.

Country house cricket, which became increasingly popular around mid-century, took the opposite line. It was determinedly amateur, without the systematic organisation that characterised League and serious club cricket. Smart uniforms, luscious refreshments and spectacular evening entertainments combined with cricket matches to make cricket party week-ends fashionable at big houses.

Umpires in this kind of cricket usually worked for the head of the house, as butler, gardener, game-keeper or stable-boy, and could operate a closed shop system with

THE OLD GIRLS' MATCH.
Small Girl (*in the School Team*). "I KNEW THERE 'D BE TROUBLE WHEN FATHER WAS ASKED TO UMPIRE. HE'S SO KEEN HE'S ALREADY NO-BALLED MOTHER TWICE."

their employers. Similar sorts of closed shops could operate all through the cricket world, especially in the small world of village cricket, but they were easiest to operate in country house cricket. There was a story popular in Kent in the 1880s of a vicar who played with his curate behind the stumps and his sexton as umpire. They were unbeatable except when they played the local mental asylum, where the doctor bowled and his head-warder umpired.

Managers of county teams had long been careful to avoid any such imputation of prejudice in connection with their teams. They were worried by the lack of a central authority to help them control discipline and codes of play, and to enforce a uniform system through all the counties. In 1879, therefore, the County Cricket Council was formed. By that time cricket was already an international game, so that all its problems in county and north/south cricket had been given a new dimension.

An English team went to America in 1859 and a Canadian team came to England. In 1869 an Aborigine team came to England, to the delight of the crowds, who enjoyed their novelty value and unpredictable style of play. In 1877 an English team went to Australia and the next year an Australian team came to England. The most important quality for umpiring international cricket played between strangers was an unmistakable air of authority, and in that respect the task was easier than umpiring county cricket, where there were problems with personal rivalries and dislikes, inherited tensions and familiar, difficult characters.

The fact that visiting teams were unknown to everyone also had its difficult side for umpires. The Australians in 1878 expressed horror at the web of class pressures they encountered and complained about its effect on umpires, even though they won their only match against England. The same complaint was made against English umpires in Philadelphia on the English tour of America, and they were booed off the pitch. With different ideas about what was cricket and what was not being wide-spread, the other main difficulty with international umpiring was to determine what style of play and behaviour was acceptable and how far players should be allowed to take their trouble-making and cajoling of umpires.

In 1884 the MCC published a new code of laws which was circulated to all the county and university clubs and also to the cricket associations of Victoria and New South Wales, Philadelphia and New York. Slowly, painfully, and increasingly resigned to the presence of umpires, cricket was becoming an officially international game with international laws.

The 1884 laws reflected the stability of the game in the previous twenty years. The only major change was that umpires were to be appointed 'one for each end', not one for each team. It was confirmation from headquarters of the principle of neutrality so often denied in practice.

Umpires needed to guard their good names jealously, as a means of keeping their jobs. As early as 1866 'Quid' wrote: 'We don't know a case where a decision has ever been dictated by a pecuniary bias; of carelessness and inattention we have jotted down hundreds.'

When the counties decided to appoint neutral umpires in 1883, they fixed a flat fee of £5 a match, irrespective of the distance the umpire had to cover, which was sometimes extremely long. Considering the cost of travelling, eating and drinking with friends after the match, and overnight accommodation for away matches, £5 was not generous. But it was an improvement on earlier fees, and it was guaranteed. At last, first class cricket umpires felt they had been accorded official dignity. They approached the late nineteenth century with their morale precarious but improved.

8

The Birth-pains of Over-arm

Umpires' powers grew like fungi in the 1880s and 1890s. There were no dramatic developments; umpires cut the same, generally unimpressive figures at the end as at the beginning of the period, but their authority expanded. In some ways it was a difficult time, with Grace at his playing peak, chucking/throwing emerging as a major problem and pad play developing as part of batting, bringing with it a major LBW problem. But in other ways it was a glorious time, with a fine flurry of amateur brilliance, the emancipation of bowling from demoralised medium pace and the establishment of international tours as regular, popular fixtures. Every age has had its difficulties for umpires, but the end of the nineteenth century had enough compensations to make it interesting and even, within limits, rewarding.

It was some comfort to be issued for the first time with an MCC book, *Instructions to Umpires*, in 1892 – a sign of official acceptance. But not everyone saw it like that. Haygarth, the formative cricket statistician and compiler of *Scores and Biographies*, complained that the modern umpire 'groans under a quantity of contentious, intricate and perplexing arrangements, combined with the new and ostentatious minor rules thrust on their shoulders continually'.

However many the new and ostentatious minor rules, they were not enough for perfectionists, who abounded then as they do now. Shortly after the MCC book was published, a batsman complained to one of the umpires in a county game about a lob bowler whose long, flapping sleeves were distracting him; was there nothing in the umpire's book of rules which covered the situation?

For better or worse, the instruction booklet became a status symbol in second class matches played by clubs ambitious for public esteem. Umpires in second class bordering on first class matches used the booklet most, to help them defend their decisions and dignify their employers. One consequence of the MCC booklet, which urged umpires to have the laws at their fingertips, was that this was the beginning of the litigious age in cricket, an age which has not yet shown any sign of coming to an end.

In 1898 Mr M. E. Pavri, the most famous Parsi cricketer, spent the summer in England, playing for the Forest Hill Cricket Club and the Surrey Cricket Club and Ground. He admitted that Parsi umpires back in India were bad, but claimed that English umpires were far from perfect, mainly because they did not always know all the laws, which he, as a visiting stranger, had taken care to learn by heart. In a game at Bournemouth Pavri was bowling and warned the batsman at his end that he was backing up too far; if he carried on going half-way down the wicket before the ball was bowled, he would be run out. The batsman ignored the warning, Pavri put the wicket down and the umpire said not out. Pavri at once produced a copy of the rules from his back pocket, opened it at the relevant section, and the umpire hastily pronounced the batsman out.

The on-the-spot expert, the bane of every umpire's life, was a late nineteenth-century apparition, eager to improve every club he visited with his knowledge of the laws. Though he might occasionally appear in village matches, on the whole he preferred the serious, ambitious ambience of local league cricket and might even, on a bad day, pop up in a first class match.

In the south, possibly less so in the north, the gap between first class and other club cricket was beginning to widen, as was the gap between first class and other club umpires. First class umpiring was a full time job, though many umpires continued to stand for their local clubs occasionally, even after becoming members of the first class circuit.

The expansion of league cricket and the formal establishment of minor counties cricket were products of this late century seriousness about cricket status. The Minor Counties Association was formed in 1895, with umpires nominated by first or second class counties and elected by minor counties' captains at a meeting chaired by the MCC secretary.

In 1901 the MCC issued an official list of umpires' signals which were used thereafter at all levels of the game, with varying degrees of orthodoxy, art and theatrical commitment.

Most MCC laws were put into practice, though often very slowly, by first and second class teams, but small clubs either ignored anything too revolutionary, or fitted it gradually into their system of play, complete with local modifications and improvements.

The number of balls in an over went up from four to five in 1889 but the five ball over was never popular; a lot of clubs ignored it and carried on with four ball overs. In 1900, after extensive consultation among first class players and umpires, which included recollections of the deceased giant Alfred Mynn declaring that as far as he was concerned the ideal over would have a hundred balls, the number of balls in an over was raised to six. All clubs at all levels accepted the six ball over eventually, and it has stayed at that number in England ever since, though Australian eight ball overs have made occasional appearances in club games and a failed first class appearance in 1939.

First class umpires in the 1880s were coming into the limelight again. The reason was a resurgence of the throwing controversy, though this time in connection with chucking rather than round-arm/over-arm. Like the earlier troubles, it produced umpiring confusion and also at least one great character umpire.

The 1880s throwing trouble was mainly confined to the first class game. All levels of cricket now had an overwhelming majority of over-arm bowlers, though there were a few round-armers, especially in the country, and just a very few under-armers, or 'lobsters'. All good umpires no-balled bowlers who bowled a variety of styles without giving notice when they changed from one to the other; that was standard umpiring practice. But there was no standard umpiring practice about what to do when a bowler was suspected of throwing.

Over-arm bowling meant faster bowling, umpires' reluctant adjustment to it, and a lingering uncertainty about actions that appeared to straighten the arm at the last minute. Umpires were unwilling to no-ball suspect bowlers, not just because of doubts about the illegality of their actions, but also for the familiar reason that the bowlers were usually ex-team mates whose livelihood was at risk.

Lancashire began the 1880s with two suspect throwers, Nash and Crossland, the latter being particularly fast and particularly suspicious. His action was denounced not only by eminent amateurs like Grace and Lord Harris, but also by a wide range of professionals, including the entire Nottinghamshire team. The summer of 1882 was wet, Crossland skittled out all the batsmen before him, Nottinghamshire refused to play Lancashire again as long as Crossland was included in their team, and not a single umpire no-balled him.

Lancashire stood by him and he went from strength to strength. On one occasion he hit a batsman on the foot with a fast yorker and the batsman left the wicket.

'You're not out!' called the umpire.

'No, but I'm going!' replied the batsman.

In August 1882, after the Lancashire/Surrey match at the Oval, *Cricket* magazine published an article about throwing which included a sardonic consideration of the umpires' position.

It is really useless to urge that the umpires are the proper judges. In the first place, there are few of them competent to decide such a point; in the second, the man who would have the courage of his opinions to no-ball anyone, in my opinion has not existed since John Lillywhite.

'Bob' Thoms, the country's leading umpire, put it more pointedly with his pronouncement 'We are not going to do anything, the gentlemen must do it.'

MCC pep-talks to umpires fell on deaf ears and it was the county teams, not the umpires, who put a stop to the early 1880s' throwing. How much they were following the lead of their gentlemen captains, as Thoms had recommended, is hard to say, but their action was clear and decisive. In December 1883 all the first class counties except Lancashire agreed not to use bowlers listed as having suspect actions.

The next year Crossland made things easier for Lancashire and for umpires everywhere by breaking the county residence qualification, living 4/5 months a year in Nottinghamshire, so getting himself disqualified from the Lancashire team.

From 1895 on, the county captains had regular meetings and when the throwing problem cropped up again in the 1890s, it was clear that umpires on their own could not and would not solve it without the county committees' help. In 1899, at the height of the throwing troubles, the MCC tried to give umpires full responsibility by giving them the power to 'call no-ball if not satisfied with the absolute fairness of any delivery'. But most umpires found they doubted whether they knew when they were doubtful.

Arthur Mold, who began playing for Lancashire in 1889, was the leading fast bowler in England by 1893 and also the most controversial, an umpire's nightmare. Grace thought his action fair, a lot of others who faced him thought his action unfair and in 1896 umpires asked captains with suspect bowlers like Mold in their teams to discipline them.

In the end, unexpectedly, it was the firm umpiring of one man which wiped the throwing problem out of cricket for the next fifty years. By the late 1890s the counties had got to the position where several of them had a suspect bowler because none of them could afford to be the only team limited to strictly fair bowlers. The January 1897 *Sporting Life* made the point that most suspect bowlers only threw by 'putting', or straightening the arm from one point, usually the elbow, which made the umpires' detection task extremely difficult.

Umpires made amends for their silence on the throwing issue by being meticulous and exacting over every other bowling fault. Thus the *Sporting Life* article could continue its commentary on umpires and throwing by remarking that 'Should a fair bowler even touch the bowler's crease when delivering a ball he is at once "called".'

This vicious circle of impotence and fussiness was broken by an Australian umpire called James Phillips who came over to England, qualified as an all-rounder for Middlesex, became an umpire and is said to have made more enemies in his six umpiring years than anyone else in the history of cricket.

Here was a character umpire without a grain of tact. He gave everyone advance notice of his opinions about bowlers, so they regarded him as prejudiced. In 1899, the year he arrived in England, he no-balled C. B. Fry, the glamorous, brilliant, conceited amateur who thrived on public admiration and was stunned that any umpire, least of all an Antipodean one, should dare take action against him.

Phillips was fresh from an anti-throwing season in Australia, where he had nipped the problem in the bud by no-balling throwers wherever he saw them; he no-balled Ernest Jones, a national hero, in a Test match. Personality and occasion meant nothing to Phillips and the tensions and social pressures of the English amateur/professional distinction bored him. He rejoiced in his image as the plain-speaking man from the outback.

Other umpires in England took heart and began to call suspect bowlers. Two more umpires no-balled Fry. In 1900 Mold was no-balled for throwing three times in one over at Trent Bridge and his captain, MacLaren, took him off for the rest of the match. That winter the county captains voted by eleven to one that Mold was an unfair bowler and drew up a list of fourteen suspect bowlers, including Mold, whom they agreed not to use.

113

Lancashire defied the ban and used Mold, whom Phillips no-balled sixteen times in ten overs in front of the Old Trafford crowd when Lancashire played Somerset. This was despite the silence of the other umpire and the boos and groans of the crowd. It was the end of Mold's cricketing career. As for Phillips, he stayed in England long enough to enjoy his outspoken reputation, then in 1905 went back to Australia to be a mining engineer. By that time throwing was no longer a cause of contention.

Phillips's handling of a difficult issue brought him gratitude, and also sharp criticism. One of the charges levelled against him was that he was a character umpire off the field as well as on, devaluing his decisions by broadcasting them. In retaliation, Phillips launched his own attacks against critics and reporters. When criticised once by a journalist about a difficult decision, he replied 'Where are you sitting? In the press box? Right, I'll come and umpire from there next innings.'

His was the opposite of the quiet style of Thoms. He did not seek to exude an air of unobtrusive authority: instead he welcomed trouble so that he could bludgeon it to death. Though unpopular with some, he was effective and, unlike his predecessor in the character umpire tradition, Caldecourt, he won his battle against the 'throwing-bowling' of his age.

For all its cavalier batsmen and its Indian summer of amateur panache, late nineteenth-century cricket needed a few toughs like Phillips to save it from becoming a matter of who could shout the loudest. By the late 1890s it was normal for pretty well the whole field to appeal for caught behind. The advice John Lillywhite gave to keepers in 1866, only one generation before, sounded like a voice from the romantic past. 'Do not ask the umpire unless you think the batsman is out; it is not cricket to keep asking the umpire questions.'

Grace set a shamelessly aggressive example with his appealing, which even extended occasionally to appealing when he was batting. In 1875, playing for the Gentlemen against the Players at the Prince's Ground, he was clean bowled but stayed where he was and

114

appealed against the decision, first hopefully, then imperiously, to both umpires. They refused to alter their verdict that he was out, citing as evidence the stumps and bails lying on the grass.

There were a number of reasons for umpires to develop stronger and tougher public images at this period: Grace, social tensions, the throwing controversy, more aggressive appealing and more outspoken press commentary on all aspects of the game, including umpires. Tom Mycroft was one of a number of umpires who eschewed an extrovert image but gave decisions with dogged determination, whatever and whoever the opposition to them. In August 1899 Straw, Worcestershire's wicket-keeper, was given out by Mycroft, 'got in A. C. Glover's way'. He was out in the same manner at Birmingham two years later. A ferocious keeper, Straw belonged to a tradition of unscrupulous appealers behind the stumps.

Concerted team appealing meant that a number of first class umpires developed thick skins which stood them in good stead when it came to pronouncing unpopular decisions. But there were still vulnerable moments. In 1901 Kent played Essex. Russell, batting for Essex, seemed to be caught at mid-off, though the fielder did not throw the ball up. So general had this practice become that its absence gave Russell hope that he had not been caught and he appealed to the umpire for a decision. Disconcerted at facing an appeal from the batsman instead of the fielding side, the umpire gave him out. In fact the fielder told his captain he had not caught it, the captain called Russell back and the umpire stood chewing his nails.

Displays of sportsmanship on that scale were rare but displays of umpiring incompetence were all too common. Despite steady improvement, English umpiring was sensitive to the pressures of group appealing and was still vulnerable to social pressures and the influence of powerful personalities on the field.

The pressures on umpires at county matches were heavy. Though umpires did not stand when their own counties were playing, local pride focussed on county cricket as a battlefield and the tensions surrounding every decision were agonising. County cricket was at its zenith in the late nineteenth century and umpires were the only participants who knew for certain before each game started that they were going to make themselves anathema with some part or other of the players and the crowd.

In 1892 the MCC agreed in principle to umpires changing their decisions if they wanted to, as long as they did it quickly, but if anything this accentuated the umpires' predicament by encouraging players to dispute decisions. Journalists added to the strain by writing up doubtful, mistaken and reversed decisions in high colour. But the most insidious strain on umpires was the quietest: the ever-growing number of laws.

Most of the late nineteenth-, early twentieth-, century laws, though onerous in their cumulative effect, were adjustments, often welcome, to laws already in existence. The enforcement of a follow-on, for example, was made optional instead of compulsory, boundaries were legally recognised, teams could make declarations instead of knocking their stumps down when they wanted to close their innings.

In 1899 the laws were amended to declare a ball 'dead' if it lodged in the batsman's clothing. This was the result of an earlier incident when William Ward, the early owner and developer of Lord's, 'played the ball into the inclosure [sic] of his pantaloons'. But the amendment inevitably made its own embarrassments. Deciding when a ball was only temporarily caught in clothing and when it was lodged in clothing was a tricky task.

There was a splendid example of umpiring imbecility on this count at Whitehaven in 1879 when G. F. Grace's XI played a local XX, including Platts of Derbyshire and Barlow, the Lancashire opener. Platts went to hit a ball and it 'stuck in his hand'. He put it in his trousers as a fielder advanced on him, and set off round the field, pursued by the entire Grace eleven, waving his bat like a club as he ran. Eventually he was held down and the

116

ball removed from his trousers, whereupon the umpire gave him not out. In fact he had been out in three ways: caught, handled the ball and obstructed the field.

Players were not the only ones with clothing that played an active part in the game. On Saturday 4 May 1889, Leicester East End were playing Knighton at Belgrave Rd Ground, Leicester and one of their batsmen hit the ball into the pocket of an elderly spectator. Either he was inside the boundary or they were running out hits because when he realised where the ball was he called out to the batsmen to run. The ball was in his lining and took a lot of getting out. The umpire rightly, but uncomfortably, resisted the fielders' attempts to get the scoring stopped while they extracted the ball.

Spectators and other natural features of the landscape were favourite sources of harassment for umpires. In small club cricket, the written rules carried less weight than local customs, and the home and away umpires' different interpretation of custom was a fertile source of trouble.

There was a match at Ipswich on Saturday 22 August 1891 between Cowell's Athletic Association and Languard Fort in which Cowell made only 19 in their first innings but declared their second at 75 for 1. This left Languard needing 58 to win, of which they had got 30 when one of their batsmen hit the ball into a tree near the pitch. Cowell's captain refused to have it called lost ball on the grounds that they could see where it was, and sent a man up the tree after it. He climbed onto a branch, got the ball and claimed a catch. The umpire gave the batsman out, the Languard batsmen refused to go on and Cowell claimed the match.

Disputes about the live or dead condition of a ball which had gone into an umpire's pocket or hit an umpire and rebounded into a fielder's hands had the same divisive effects. Difficult situations often produced hair-raising decisions like 'I didn't see it, but I give him out' (umpire of a Saturday club match between Royton and Littleborough, Lancashire), and were one of the reasons

117

league cricket increased its popularity in the north in the 1890s.

The neutral umpires of league cricket, on whose performance both sides wrote reports after each game, were free of the charge of local bias in difficult situations. Following the lead of the Birmingham and District League, the North Staffordshire League was founded in 1889, the Lancashire League in 1890, the Huddersfield League in 1891, the Bradford League in 1903. From that day to this, league cricket has maintained that its umpires are better than non-league umpires because they have to be good to keep their jobs. It is impossible to say for certain whether early league umpires justified this claim but they do seem to have been respected more by the players, who expected more of them.

But even the best umpires sometimes had more of a sense of duty to the public than to cricketing propriety. 'Bob' Thoms once gave Jessop not out in a match at the Hastings festival though he was clearly run out by yards. The bowler complained about the decision and Thoms replied 'Sixpenny gate, holiday crowd. Can't disappoint 'em. But near thing, sir, very near thing.'

It was this whimsicality of cricket, often serenely inattentive to its wealth of laws, that bemused the few foreigners who came to England in the late nineteenth century and watched cricket. Gaston Berlemont, a young Frenchman who had come to England for romantic reasons, published a series of articles from Paris in 1895, of which the fifth was about a cricket match.

> . . . It seems that 22 men and 2 judges called umpires take part, the 22 men are divided into 2 teams of 11 under a capitaine. One complete team 'takes the field' and plays against only 2 men of the other team, which means they are outnumbered by 5½ to 1, not counting the 2 umpires. . . . at the side of each wicket stands an umpire rendered completely incognito by a heavy disguise of hats, coats and jerseys . . . suddenly it was 'over'. At least, I distinctly heard one of the secretive umpires say it was, but it was not over. Some players changed position . . . Someone then tells an umpire that it is raining. For some reason I have yet to find out

umpires can never tell when it's raining, or even getting dark, on their own. Someone else must always tell them, but it means nothing because it is tea-time, and so 'Bails off for tea' is the cry.

But even the tea interval, poor Monsieur Berlemont's only respite from the incomprehensibility of cricket in general and umpires in particular, was contentious. In 1901 there were protests against the existence of a tea interval at all and in 1903 Essex tried to have it abolished. The Warwickshire captain, H. W. Bainbridge, supported by most other county captains, made sure it was retained because it often helped to break long stands. Every single umpire in first class cricket wanted the tea interval retained, but their opinion was only sought as a last ditch resource in case players were too divided in their views to reach a clear majority verdict.

Umpires only really came into their own as advisers and consultants to the law makers when there were not clear and consistent laws for them to enforce. For the most part, their power was inconsistent and individual.

Another end-of-century problem emerged to emphasise this fact. Until the 1880s LBW was of minor importance in cricket; it only accounted for one in 40 first class wickets and was often ignored altogether in village and small club cricket. But from about 1885 on it grew steadily more important until by the mid 1920s it accounted for one in 9 first class wickets, was accepted as a fair means of dismissal at all levels of cricket and was a major torment for umpires.

The leg play denounced as 'shabby' by Beldham and Nyren had always been unpopular. If it got the batsman out, that was what he deserved. This attitude survived until well into the nineteenth century, by which time leg play had become much more common. Ted Wainwright, the great Yorkshire all-rounder of the 1890s and early 1900s, once bowled ten men in a county match and was asked why they hadn't padded him away. They could have done so with impunity because his deliveries pitched outside the off stump and cut back; an LBW decision at that time required the ball to pitch in line

119

between wicket and wicket. He explained that padding the ball away would have been 'contrary to aesthetic morality'.

Arthur Shrewsbury dedicated himself to making the aesthetic morality of cricket a thing of the past. He was a Nottinghamshire batsman who began the 1885 season by padding away everything that would have hit the wicket. The new prosperity of bowling, with its off-breaks and over-arm speed, was padded to a standstill. Bowlers could do nothing about it.

The MCC, sensitive to charges of changing and adding to the laws too often, did not think the problem merited a change of law and asked players, county committees and umpires between them to put an end to the evil. But it was one thing to discourage leg play and quite another to stop it. Within five years leg play was in general use and the MCC was officially alarmed to debate a proposed new law declaring a batsman out LBW if he played the ball with his legs and it would have hit the wicket, regardless of where it pitched. The chief argument against it was that deciding where the ball would have gone after bouncing was too much of a burden for umpires. There would be even more appeals, bullying and resentment. The change failed to get the necessary two-thirds majority and the old law was retained, though no one was happy with it. The minor counties tried out a change of law.

It was an unsatisfactory trial; it only reflected minor counties' opinion, not first class counties' opinion, and umpires' views were not canvassed. Inspired by this impasse, the Rev. Jones of Crowborough, Sussex, delivered a sermon in March 1903 on LBW, a 'parable of the cricket field', text Matthew XIII, 34. ('All this Jesus said to the crowd in parables; indeed, he said nothing to them without a parable.')

Visitors to England were always bemused by the mystical, almost religious status of cricket in the eyes of its serious fans, especially amateurs. Umpires should have been the mysterious embodiments of power held in reverence by all. Occasionally they may have been, but only in amateur, old-fashioned or consciously romantic games. In 1904 A. G. Steel and Hon R. H. Lyttleton wrote this about umpires: 'First class amateur cricketers should remember that it is impossible for them to pay too much deference to the decisions of umpires, as it is from them that the standard or tone of morality in the game is taken.'

Everyday reality was different. For the most part, as W. E. W. Collins, an old country cricketer, remembered in his diary just after the turn of the century, umpires were 'the most abused class of men in England'. The choice of umpire in village matches was influenced by 'a man's fighting weight and capacity', not by the aura of omniscient serenity he exuded. Village cricket was then, as it is today, unromantic and utilitarian. Collins remembered how an umpire in the 1870s and 80s was commonly regarded as the most useful man on his side.

Nevertheless, the romantic image survived in the form of ceremonial umpires' clothes for special matches. The late nineteenth century Whit Monday derby between Collins's village of Radley, Oxfordshire and the neighbouring village boasted umpires dressed like undertakers: tall hats, black coats and white ties. They each held a long white stick, borrowed from the church, where it was used to rap unruly boys on Sundays. Batsmen had to touch the stick to score a run. Tradition dies hard in country cricket.

Being used to the old under-arm bowling, Collins was surprised to see round-arm bowling, even at the end of the century, but not as surprised as the umpire. The first ball bowled in the Whit Monday match hit the batsman in the eye and the umpire, without any appeal being made, called 'hout' then, to shouts of laughter from all round the ground, 'leg afront'. Buoyed up by the dignity of his office, he went down the pitch waving his stick at the batsman, who walked off, leaving his bat behind in mute protest. The umpire adjusted his white tie.

Village cricket was then and is now the last bastion of ignorance and bigotry, personal and social vendettas,

121

local pride, local customs and local attachment to the way things used to be. Only village cricket could have produced this unselfconscious comment at the turn of the century, made by a Cotswold landowner looking to cricket as a rock of stability in a changing world and revealing something of the village social system in which umpires still had to operate: 'When I went on to bowl left-handed donkey-drops, Tom Peregrine (my own servant, if you please) was very near no-balling me.'

9

The International Game

Harry Bagshaw of Derbyshire was so devoted to umpiring that when he died in 1927 he was buried, as he had requested, in his umpire's white coat, holding a cricket ball in his hand. He could not face heavenly judgement without the emblems of cricket judgement to fortify him. Bagshaw was one of many umpires early this century who did not take just his job seriously, but also its trappings, rituals and little bits and pieces. By the 1930s being a first class umpire was more than a serious occupation; it was a very serious occupation, and for the first time umpires became famous for being good umpires, not character or controversial ones, though there were always one or two of those around.

In 1900 a reader of *Cricket* magazine wrote to the editor saying that although he thought first class umpiring was much better than it had been a few years before, it still left a lot to be desired. What he wanted to see was the establishment of an umpiring college where the job would be treated as a profession, complete with the appropriate ties, blazers, qualification ceremonies and the sort of reverence Harry Bagshaw was later to show for his white coat. This would make it attractive to public school boys and varsity graduates. At the moment there was no-one of this type in umpiring, but if the profession made use of its new seriousness it would become acceptable to the upper middle class as a job on a par with stock-broking and chartered accountancy.

Although early twentieth century umpires in first class, league and serious club cricket were ex-players pretty well to a man, and were familiar, if not always accurately, with the laws, this did not give umpiring a professional status. But it did distinguish English first class umpires from their counterparts abroad, who umpired during time off work and were generally agreed to be less good at their job. When W. E. W. Collins wrote his *Leaves from an Old Country Cricketer's Diary* in 1908 he described cheerfully the eccentricities of umpiring in Ireland: 'The native umpiring in Ireland appealed to me on the whole as combining impartiality with a cheerful indifference to facts and criticism.'

Village cricket was the last English home for umpires who had never played cricket and were spectacularly ignorant of its rules. The only other kind of cricket which could produce such incompetent and partisan umpires was country house cricket, which might be good enough to feature the odd first class player but at the same time light-hearted enough to include incompetent family friends.

The first world war crippled country house cricket and widened still further the gap between first class and every other kind of cricket. Countless villages, clubs and leagues simply ceased to exist as cricket communities.

When the tally of war casualties was taken, it did not include umpires, but if it had, it would have shown that they were the only group in cricket which increased its numbers. Players needed to be extremely fit; most umpires only needed to be fit enough to stand and concentrate for a day, get into position and out of the way when required, and remember the ever-expanding body of cricket laws. Wounded ex-servicemen keen to stay involved with the game made ideal umpires.

Frank Chester lost an arm in the war, ending his brilliantly promising county career with Worcestershire when he was only eighteen. He started umpiring first class matches in 1922, when he was twenty-six, twenty years younger than most other first-class umpires. His general health was good and he always rated basic good health as the number one necessity for umpires. In 1919 county cricket picked up its life where the war had cut it off, and started by trying two-day instead of three-day matches. Umpires as well as players complained that the longer hours necessary each day were too exhausting, physically and mentally, and the experiment was abandoned.

County cricket recovered after the war far better than anyone had expected, though its scars were apparent. Batsmen carried on longer than they would have done if there had been a new generation of young batsmen to oust them. Jack Hobbs was 35 in 1918 and carried on in first class cricket for another 18 years. Frank Woolley began playing for Kent in 1906 and did not retire until he was 51.

Bowlers lasted less well than batsmen. Barnes, the slow medium bowler who had dominated international cricket before the war, was 45 when it was over and, unlike some batting contemporaries, felt too old to go on. Consequently bowling was a major weakness in English cricket until well into the 1920s and the low standard of English cricket as a whole was shown when England lost eight Tests in a row in 1920–1.

But cricket clubs proliferated; the Minor Counties Championship restarted in 1920; school, university, league and village cricket resumed, though sometimes weakly; only country house cricket had suffered so badly that it never recovered. As for umpires, they abounded and umpiring standards rose. Only village and small club cricket still had room for bumbling old umpires whom everyone liked and no-one respected.

Even before the war, umpiring seriousness was developing into earnestness. Knowles Pfeiffer, the captain of Barnsley from 1904 to 14, wrote an appreciation of Yorkshire umpiring which, as every Yorkshireman knew, had always been serious business, at all levels of the game:

> The umpiring is very good, very strict as to times of starting and time allowed for batsmen to come to the wicket. I have often known an umpire to hold a watch in his hand . . . The spectators are very fine judges of the game and never miss even a fine point.

The remarks about timing are typically twentieth

century. Cheap watches added timing to the list of umpiring concerns. Timed out was never a comfortable decision to give against a batsman and umpires disliked it. In the 1919 game between Sussex and Somerset at Taunton, Sussex needed one run to win and their last batsman, R. B. Heygate, who was crippled with rheumatism and had not been expecting to bat, had to crawl to the wicket. When he got there, wincing with pain, one of the Somerset fielders appealed against him under the two minutes rule and the umpire had to give him out. J. C. White, the Somerset captain, was too embarrassed to do anything about it. The umpire pulled up the stumps and marched straight off, unable to bear the sight of poor Heygate making his painful way back to the pavilion.

Most umpires never had to cope with that level of ruthlessness. It was one of the results of the increasing pressure operating in first class cricket. In December 1907 county captains kept up the pressure with two new demands of umpires. They were reasonable demands; it was the captains' act of putting them in writing and making them official that indicated the new gravity in first class cricket. Every umpire had to have written testimony of his fitness and good eyesight, but it was officially agreed that spectacles were not a bar to umpiring.

Alex Skelding, one of the great character umpires who emerged alongside the great functional umpires after the first world war, wore spectacles. They were the reason he failed a Leicestershire county trial as a fast bowler, though he bowled very well, and even in 1931, when he became a first class umpire with his sight and fitness officially approved, he suffered the odd crack from bowlers about his eyesight. 'Where's your guide dog?' a batsman once asked him on being given out. 'Oh him?' replied Skelding, 'I got rid of him for yapping', then with an imperious wave of his hand, 'as was ever my wont'.

Skelding was the *enfant terrible* of umpiring between the wars, resurrecting the Caldecourt style of extrovert umpiring. He umpired a lot of county matches but was thought too risky for a Test match. He had worked on a racecourse for a while and sometimes gave signals to the scorers in tic-tac. The Australians liked him. He wore large white boots, as Australian umpires often did, and carried on the old cricketing/drinking alliance the Australians had always found sympathetic. He carried a flask in his pocket which he said 'keeps out the cold and helps me to see straight'.

Village cricket clung proudly to its inheritance of keeping out the cold. Pictures of Skelding, a dramatic figure with his red nose and shock of white hair, were a not uncommon adornment on the walls of country cricketing pubs. The George Hotel in Henfield, Sussex, was one among innumerable hotels and pubs throughout the country which had long been the traditional venue for the cricket club's ordinary after the match. The George was the club headquarters in the eighteenth century and for most of the nineteenth century, when it lent its field for matches. In 1920 it set itself up again after the war as the official club headquarters. It took more than war to break up the marriage of cricket and drink, and Skelding delighted in helping to keep the marriage happy.

He was good at cultivating his image and revelled in the attention it brought him. In a world equipped with radio and, by the late 1930s with television too, he saw no reason for umpires to keep themselves out of the public eye. A media umpire, he barked rather than spoke his answers to appeals. He perfected his notoriety by publishing a poem called 'Duties, Trials and Troubles of County Cricket Umpires'. The duties came a long way second to the trials and troubles.

— Most of the time he stands to be shot at;
An immobile creature for mankind to pot at.

Umpires' low pay and the insecurity of their job, from which they could be removed if they got three adverse reports from county captains, were constant causes of complaint. Between the wars umpires earned £200 a year for standing in an average of twenty matches. It was a struggle to live, with no winter work and no expenses paid. Chester was outspoken against umpires' grim conditions because he began umpiring very young and knew that with only one hand he had no prospect of alternative or supplementary work. He umpired with fanatical concentration, determined not to lose his job.

He said later that the old umpires did not like him being so serious about the job; it made them feel threatened. In one of his first county matches Chester gave both captains out on the first day and was told by the other umpire as they walked off that he would not last long as an umpire. 'If you give skippers out, you sign your own death warrant.'

Chester was a first class umpire for the next thirty-three years, umpiring more Test matches than anyone else before or since. He set a new standard in umpiring.

Not all first class umpires were paragons. On one occasion 'Razor' Smith, the Surrey bowler, got three batsmen LBW at Cheltenham, then had a plumb LBW refused. When he asked the umpire why it was not out, the umpire replied with disarming honesty: 'Well, I've already given three out, and I can't give any more out just yet.'

Umpiring according to more exalted principles was hard work. Chester nearly gave it up because he found it so much more exhausting and less rewarding than playing. His rapport with players, like that of all English umpires, was close; the older players helped and advised him, but he felt he was on the outside looking in. His consolation was that he was still part of the game he loved.

English umpires were generally thought of as the best in the world, though by no means perfect. There is no such thing as a perfect umpire. Chester made his decisions slowly, thoughtfully and well, but there were some players, especially Australians, who thought he fell victim to public admiration in later years and sometimes bent the rules to play to the crowd, becoming anti-Australian in the process. In the 20s and 30s, however, international opinion was unanimous in praising English umpires in general and Frank Chester in particular.

In the late 1920s first class umpires like Chester had far more international cricket to handle than ever before. As well as the established Test fixtures against Australia and South Africa, the West Indies sent their first Test team to England in 1928; New Zealand in 1929–30, India in 1932. In response, English teams went on far more tours than ever before; players welcomed the winter money and by 1930 English cricket was vigorous and widely travelled. Umpires were the only participants in the game who always got left at home.

England's prime opponent was Australia, armed from 1928 on with its ballistic weapon, Bradman. He first came to England in 1930, when he was twenty-two, and averaged 139 in the Test matches and 98.66 in the whole tour. The MCC tour of Australia in 1932–3, the infamous 'bodyline' series, was played in the shadow of Bradman's formidable talent, which was an understandable, if inexcusable, reason for bowling to terrorise and incapacitate.

Where Bradman was concerned, the bowling seemed to have achieved both objectives even before the first Test, at Sydney, had been played. He felt so run down that doctors told him to rest and he did not play until the second Test at Melbourne, where he was bowled first ball by a bouncer.

The tour was horrific for the Australian umpires. Legally, bodyline bowling could not be faulted except under the 'fair and unfair play' rule. But by the third Test in Adelaide anti-English feeling had risen to fever pitch and a squad of police was called in and kept behind the stand in case there was a riot. Larwood's short-pitched, fast bowling straight at the body, with a packed leg-side field to catch deflected balls, won the match for England by 338 runs. There were furious arguments about who should put an end to this kind of bowling, which was 'not cricket' – umpires, captains and individual bowlers were called upon to take action.

Being the 'sole judges of fair and unfair play', the

umpires were under pressure from the Australians to stop England's bodyline tactic, and from Jardine, the English captain, to leave it alone as legitimate, aggressive cricket. Frank Chester wrote in his autobiography that he could see nothing in the laws to prevent this kind of bowling and he thought Larwood an unusually fair bowler who never appealed without good cause. Frank Lee, another great English umpire, who started his career in 1931, thought bumpers and bouncers unfair. It was a knotty problem.

England won the series 4–1, amid bitterly hostile feelings, and a year later the MCC decided that, like umpire Lee, a good number of Englishmen and the entire population of Australia, it thought bodyline bowling 'not cricket'. It passed this resolution at the end of the 1933 season: 'That any form of bowling which is obviously a direct attack by the bowler upon the batsman would be an offence against the spirit of the game.'

The following winter the MCC had mercy on umpires and added a definition of direct attack bowling and pledged support to umpires who took action against it under the 'fair and unfair play' law.

The county captains and the Imperial Cricket Conference accepted these proposals. Umpires sighed philosophically. The bodyline tour had dramatically demonstrated their isolation when dealing with bowling problems. After the 1932–3 season Bradman studied the laws of cricket and passed the New South Wales umpires' exam, not in order to become an umpire; he was in his full glory as a batsman, but 'to learn about the game'. How influential bodyline was in deciding him on this course is impossible to guess. Bradman had always been interested in cricket from the umpires' point of view and made it clear that he respected umpires.

By the 1930s, English umpires thought of themselves as deserving of respect. Although the civil servants of cricket, they always numbered a few characters amongst them. Bill Reeves of Essex was a very good all-rounder and, after he retired, a very good umpire. Not quiet by nature, he was famous for his repartee, on and off the

130

field. He told a selector he and Frank Chester could choose a better side than the selectors, but he would need £1,000 from a Sunday paper before disclosing who his choices would be. Obviously umpires could give newspapers and radio a priceless inside view of cricket, but it was usually part of their silent civil service image not to do so.

Basking in international recognition of their importance, they developed confidence. As early as 1912 a club match between Bootle and Sefton in Lancashire had given rise to a lot of literature about umpires' status, which became a big issue throughout the game. In this match the umpire had given the striker out LBW, the striker protested that he had touched the ball and the captain of the bowling side let him go on batting. The Lancashire cricket writer, G. A. Brooking, took up the umpire's cause, unconcerned with the rights or wrongs of his decision:

> Except in a most glaring case of error, an umpire's decision should never be over-ruled, and even then only with the consent of the umpire. . . . Some captains take too much upon themselves in this respect, without any thought to the feelings of the umpire, who is there to give decisions.

LBW was still a bed of nettles for umpires and in 1933 an experiment was tried which would have gladdened the Bootle and Sefton umpire's heart – a batsman could be out LBW even if he had snicked the ball before it hit his legs. Umpires reported that it encouraged bowlers and was easy to operate. Nevertheless it was abandoned after one year. In 1937, after repeated attempts, the law was changed to allow an umpire to give a batsman out if the ball bounced outside the off stump, as long as it hit the striker between wicket and wicket.

From 1933 on, Bradman had been supporting this idea because 'it establishes the whole groundwork for batting and bowling'. Frank Chester voted against the change because he thought it would base LBW convictions on artificial assessments. In general, umpires' attitudes to the new law can best be described as resigned.

Bowler (his sixth appeal for an obvious leg-before). " 'Ow's that?"
Umpire (drawing out watch). "Well, he's been in ten minutes
now–Hout!"

Any attempt at improvement was welcome, though it
would probably raise as many problems as it solved.

The very fact that umpires had been asked what they
thought was enough to upset some people, who thought
umpires' powers were already growing too fast. One
sports writer wrote an attack in 1940 on the 'ever-
growing and encroaching powers of umpires'. He was
particularly incensed because he thought selectors,
goaded perhaps by Bill Reeves' boast about his selecting
ability, were consulting umpires. What, he wrote
fiercely, would happen if an umpire was asked his
opinion of a bowler who happened to have been
complaining about his decisions? He rightly foresaw a
time when umpires would become advisors to the selectors and even, eventually, become selectors themselves.

LBW became a worse problem for umpires with the
advent of swing bowling, which was beginning to
flourish at about this time. Wicket surfaces were better
than they had ever been and swinging or swerving
bowling was a bowler's device to break through the
batting hegemony of the 1920s and 1930s. In 1902 the
line of the crease had been lengthened by 2' to 8' 8",
which helped swing bowlers and the growing eclipse of

spin bowlers. A wider crease made run out and stumping decisions easier.

A little light relief in first class cricket was longed for and hard to come by. There were precious few of the local eccentricities and special rules for special grounds' which had always adorned village cricket. It was a joy when Goddard of Gloucestershire, fielding at mid-off in a match against Sussex in August 1932, stopped the ball with his cap and umpire Parry awarded the batsman, Melville, five runs. It gave the cricketing brain bank a deliciously minor adjustment to make to the laws, and one on which international relations were unlikely to founder – the five-run penalty should be added to the runs scored for the shot, not substituted for them.

The theatrical potential of umpiring meant that its

HOT WEATHER—UMPIRE AND CLOTHES-HORSE.

first class seriousness could never totally asphyxiate. Even Chester developed mannerisms. He signalled leg-byes melodramatically, though like most umpires he thought they should be abolished. He tossed up the first of his six counting stones with exaggerated, sad delight, looking at it as if it was a cricket ball. Though straight-faced to the point of gloom by comparison with Skelding and Reeves, he did not mind causing the odd laugh.

On one occasion he was umpiring at the bowler's end in a Surrey/Sussex local derby. Langridge, the bowler, liked the umpire close to the wicket and Chester liked to bend forward with his head on a level with the bails. Langridge bowled a half-volley and the batsman, F. R. Brown of Surrey, smashed it back straight into Chester's false arm, knocking it right out of its socket. It bounced once and went crashing into the sightscreen. There was stricken silence all round the ground at the sight of an arm lying on the grass. Chester left and got it refitted, then came back and ostentatiously stood yards behind the stumps, to the relief and delight of the crowd.

On the whole, first class umpires had more to be cheerful about in the twentieth century than they had had before, but they also had more responsibilities and a more demanding public. When A. E. Trott, the Australian and Middlesex batsman and for a short while Middlesex umpire, died in 1914, *The Times* wrote a long obituary which said that one of the reasons for his suicide – he shot himself – was that he was a personality in an age of automata. 'In older days there were many more of the class that may be called 'characters' and Trott was essentially one of those.'

He was famous as the first man to hit a ball over the pavilion at Lord's and achieved another record in getting a hat trick of wickets twice in an innings, one of the hat tricks being part of an astonishing spell, taking four wickets in four balls. Trott was forty-two years old when he died and had been a patient at St. Mary's Hospital, Harlesden, for some time. It was too sad an end to leave as the last word on Trott. For the purposes of this book the simplest tribute was the last sentence of *The Times* obituary: 'In the last year or two he had been a first class umpire and had proved himself a most capable one.'

10

The Quiet Old Days

The 1940s and 1950s were a quiet era in cricket. Compared to what was to come, the years just after the war were subdued. But they held some substantial problems for umpires because they saw a resurrection of the throwing menace.

Most retired umpires who remember the 1940s and 1950s do not pick out throwing as a significant feature of the time. It was largely confined to first class cricket and did not make more than its usual random impact on the other levels of the game. Instead, almost every umpire picks out players' attitude to the game as the quality that changed most and had the most impact.

Cricketers' attitudes can be difficult to assess, but umpires who worked in the 1940s and 1950s obviously do feel that players were more fraught than before, and more exclusively committed to winning. John Paddon, who umpired for years between the wars for Gloucester City and Oxford City clubs, found it a sad experience after the war because he watched the players become steadily more set on winning, at the expense of everything else. This is what umpires from the post-war years often remember.

But not always. Village cricket has always been one of the strongholds of village patriotism but a lot of local loyalty was drained away by the greater social mobility of life after the war. The Roses matches in the 20s were notoriously savage and only mellowed after the war, when people moved more freely in and out of the two counties involved and were less emotional in their support.

Neither players nor spectators can ever have been as hell-bent on victory as when they staked huge sums of money on it except possibly in international cricket, which did not exist in cricket's gambling days and quickly generated a surfeit of intensity, not to say bitterness, from the 30s onwards. This was especially true of the England/Australia Tests.

George Mikes, a Hungarian who was in London during the Munich crisis, wrote incredulously about the English attitude to cricket in the shadow of war. 'We – journalists, refugees, foreigners – were discussing the chances of peace and war, and the dangers of appeasement; our English friends rushed to the telephone or the radio and reported to each other that Australia were 279 for 5, that Hammond was out for a duck and incomprehensible things like that . . . I saw a huge headline in the *Evening Standard*: "England in Danger!" I rushed to buy a newspaper to find that there was some difficulties in the Test match . . .'

In 1946, the Australians overwhelmed post-war England. Chester umpired in the 1948 Australian tour of England and took the unprecedented step of saying publicly that he disapproved of the Australians over-appealing, with gestures and jumping about, and deplored their habit of making LBW appeals from the covers. He received floods of letters, most of them supporting him and regretting the way Test match appealing was becoming so belligerent.

The Australians had not been driven to these tactics out of need. With Bradman batting and Miller bowling superbly, they won four of the five Tests and did not lose a single match on the tour. Chester reckoned that, in the end, the Australians were always keener to win than the English. But now they had a rival: the West Indies, where cricket playing was fanatical. When England toured the West Indies in 1953–4, Perry Burke, one of the series umpires, had his life threatened and his family accosted and intimidated on the day he gave the Jamaican Holt out LBW for 94. The tour ended in a draw.

After the war more Test matches were played annually than before, and they were more widely publicised. With the growing popularity of other sports, in particular football, athletics and tennis, cricket needed all the help it could get, and the pressure which the new publicity put on players and umpires was part of the price to be paid for keeping the game going.

While Test cricket drew huge crowds, county and league cricket attracted vast numbers of spectators to pay its way. The Roses matches, even in the 40s, when they may have been past their passionate peak, were like county matches in gaining capacity crowds. Between the wars the north had reigned supreme in county cricket. Beating the best of the southern counties was a popular triumph but the great northern derby was a major holiday event. After the War, however even Yorkshire and Lancashire, with their dedicated followers, lost some to rival sports, new jobs and other distractions. They had money troubles like every other team.

All levels of cricket, from village to Test match, had to fight to finance themselves after the war. Cricket balls were put on the rationing list, to the amazement of foreign diplomats, who continued to regard cricket as the home of English madness. Because of the shortage of cricket balls, it was decided in 1947 that new balls no longer had to be provided at the start of every innings. Only first class cricket had taken the new ball regulation absolutely seriously anyway, and in some club and village matches balls continued to be used until they were beaten badly out of shape and out of their stitching. The first of a stream of alterations was made to the length of time a ball should be used before being changed: the limit was to be 55 overs, not 200 runs as before.

Everything in post-war cricket was seen in bowling terms. It was a bowlers' age, just as the years between the wars had been a batsmens' age. One of umpires' main jobs in the 1950s and 1960s was to stop bowlers pulling up the seams of balls, especially as swing and seam bowling became more common. Watchful umpires

138

BATSMAN (*taking guard*): "*What guard is that, umpire?*" RUSTIC
UMPIRE: "*You can't better it. sur.*" BATSMAN (*getting irate*): "*But what is it. Centre, middle and leg or what* RUSTIC UMPIRE: "*Well, I be blessed if I know.*"

smelled the ball often, so that batsmen would not try greasing it or putting salve on it. Swing and swerve bowling produced defensive batting, which obliged umpires to develop prolonged powers of concentration.

The most spectacular demonstration of this umpiring asset did not come from England; it was wrung out of the umpires in a match at Poona in the 1948–9 season. They had to endure day after day in the heat while B. B. Nimbalkar of Maharasashtra made his remorseless way to 443 not out. He was all set to break Bradman's world record of 452 not out but the other side, Kathiawar, refused to go on, preferring to concede the match. The journalist who reported the match was too comatose with boredom to mention the umpires, who they were or how they kept themselves awake during the ordeal.

In England too, defensive batting made for boring cricket, though not as magnificently boring as Nimbalkar's effort. It was no fun umpiring first class matches in front of small crowds with only an occasional appeal for LBW off a swerving ball to interrupt the uneventful overs. Alex Skelding wrote a report on his benefit match when he retired from playing, which began with characteristic humour: 'Play began in a biting wind before a sparse crowd.'

Like all umpires, Skelding was glad when the change came in 1947 from umpires pitching the wicket to the captain of the home side pitching the wicket. This had long been the practice anyway. Although umpires still had the responsibility of checking that this had been done properly, at least one small duty had been lifted off their shoulders.

Village and club cricket recovered more quickly from the war than county cricket; their organisers did not depend on public, only local support, and they did not have such heavy expenses. Many village and club umpires remained happily oblivious of the new correctness which even village crowds were coming to expect of them. In general, however, the trend towards law-abiding and conventional umpires continued to develop.

Chester reckoned that despite the new wave of post-war aggressive appealing, the justness of appeals rose with the class of cricket. Village and small club appeals were often absurd and called forth absurd decisions from umpires, such as the 'out, got in the way of the ball' immortalised on the scorecard of a Cotswold club after the war.

Clubs which took themselves seriously tried to enforce more rigorous standards. James Payne umpired for Shepherd's Bush Cricket Club for thirty years. In one game in the 1940s, towards the end of his long term of office, he got fed up with a new member who appealed every time the ball hit the batsman on the leg. Finally he said: 'Not out, sir, and gentlemen of the Shepherd's Bush Cricket Club do not appeal for things like that.'

The trouble was that they probably did, as did most club cricketers. The 1947 LBW law confirmed that a batsman could be out if he was hit, leg before wicket, by a ball which would have hit the stumps, provided it pitched in line with the stumps or outside the off stump. Umpires had to get used to judging LBW off swing bowling, though few of them liked it.

Frank Lee was one of the post-war generation of umpires, weaned on the example of Frank Chester, and he adopted Chester's 'low' stance, head level with the bails, to make the judging of height in LBW easier. He was one of the many umpires who disliked the LBW law because it killed leg spin bowling; it was impossible for leg spinners to get a favourable decision. Lee thought there were fewer class batsmen than there had been when he watched big matches as a boy in the 1920s, and he thought the LBW law encouraged medium pace swing bowling and cautious, defensive batting.

Lee belonged to the school of silent umpiring; he believed the ideal umpire was unobtrusive, and he only published his views on cricket after his retirement. He was not a character umpire like Skelding, nor was he as famous as Chester. But he was an umpire of the television age and, though he avoided controversy and kept a low profile on the field, he believed in contributing as much as he could to the game by appearing on sports quiz panels, speaking at dinners and giving lectures and talks.

Frank Lee came from a typical post-war umpiring background. His father was a greengrocer and the whole family was cricket mad. They were Middlesex supporters and he used to get up early to help his father with the marketing while they argued about cricket. On free mornings, he and his brothers and friends played cricket or football before school. In 1922 he got a job on the Lord's groundstaff, sweeping the stands, selling match cards and, in his time off, meeting his idols, Jack Hobbs and Frank Chester. It is a measure of Chester's eminence that, even as a mere umpire, he figured in a young cricket fan's pantheon.

After two seasons at Lord's Lee became a nets bowler. It was desperately hard finding winter work and when his mother died and his father closed down the family business, he accepted an offer from Somerset and became one of their openers. He stayed there until the war and in 1948 applied to Lord's for a position as umpire. With the recommendation of Chester, who was at the height of his eminence and had just become the only umpire ever to be awarded a testimonial fund, he was elected onto the panel of first class umpires.

Lee never made much money out of umpiring, any more than Chester or any other first class umpire did. Until the 1950s umpires had to pay their expenses out of their meagre wages. One umpire turned up the night before a county match in 1946, when the physical hardships of travel were even worse than the financial ones, and had to sleep in an air-raid shelter because he could not find anywhere he could afford to stay. The shelter was already being used as a hotel by an amateur who was going to play in the same match. In the middle of the night they were joined by a sports writer assigned to cover the match.

By this time professional umpires had a strong, if strange, *esprit de corps*, torn between identifying with players and, as the air raid shelter episode implies, identifying with the non-playing world of cricket culture: writers, journalists, broadcasters, groundsmen. As English first class umpires were the only ones in the world who were ex-players, they were the only ones who had this feeling of belonging but at the same time of being on the outside looking in.

Some umpires never felt excluded. Eddie Paynter, the great Lancashire and England left-hander of the 1930s, became an umpire when he stopped playing but met so many of his old playing pals that he had to give it up because he couldn't afford the drinking. Paul Gibb, who solved his accommodation problems by going round the cricket circuit in a caravan, gave up umpiring for the same reason.

But most first class umpires were ambivalent about their job. Chester almost gave it up because he found it painfully nostalgic, but he loved it too much to stop. There is a built-in nostalgia about umpiring. Umpires are sentimental creatures. Even Chester, who was a tough character, kept all his life the six stones he had dug out of his garden for his first county match, Essex v Somerset at Leyton in 1922. He kept them in a matchbox during the winter.

John Paddon, the Oxford and Gloucester umpire, said club umpires felt as miserable as first class umpires at not really being members of their teams. He thought the worst moment in a day's umpiring was the close of play, when everyone went off to the pub and the umpires were left behind on their own.

The winter months were bleak for umpires, emotionally and financially. But umpires were not the only people who found cricket hard to fit in with earning a living. The amateurs of the early years of the century, who enlivened many a match with their impromptu displays of carefree batting, were a dying breed. This gave the Gentlemen v Players fixture a poignant attraction; even, or perhaps especially, in the serious, worried, post-war years the annual Gentlemen v Players fixture at Lord's drew huge crowds – over 28,000 in 1948. That particular match was won for the Players by Len Hutton, who scored a magnificent century.

It was the dawning of a new age when Hutton, although a professional, was elected captain of England in 1952. The few umpires who expressed an opinion about the old distinction between professionals and amateurs all said they were glad to see it go. They missed, as everyone missed, the presence of the odd aristocratic amateur in a professional team, but they did not at all miss the faint touch of class pressure it put on umpires, who were all lower-middle or working class.

It was not just the fact of an amateur's superior wealth and class which could unsettle umpires; it was the associ-

143

ated paraphanalia. Gentlemen and Players came out of the pavilion by different gates. At Worcester, the Gentlemen changed out of their boots at lunch and went to a hotel near the ground, leaving the Players to eat the club food. By the 50s, such distinctions were becoming fewer, to the general relief of umpires.

Not that Players were personally easier than Gentlemen for umpires to handle. Hutton was a dour Yorkshireman who looked on a dismissal as a personal assault. By the 1950s he had a big following among young cricketers, who admired his batting skill and dogged temperament. It took a brave umpire to give a difficult decision against him. But by then England had a good supply of brave umpires.

In 1951 Hutton was batting for England against South Africa at the Oval when he swept at Athol Rowan's off-break, which hit him on the glove and went up in the air behind him. He waved his bat at it, preventing Russell Endean, the South African keeper, from catching it, and it fell harmlessly to the ground. Endean appealed to the bowler's end umpire, Dai Davies, for obstruction, and he gave Hutton out, with the approval of Chester at square leg. Hutton claimed he had only been trying to stop the ball hitting his wicket, which would have been legal. But as the ball had hit him on the glove, it would have been a catch if Hutton had not obstructed it and Davies scored moral points for giving the correct, but exceptional and unpopular decision. It kept the newspapers happy for days.

Most umpires preferred to stay out of the limelight, but the occasional bit of controversial publicity undeniably had its attractions. David Sheppard, who played for England on and off in the 1950s and later became the Bishop of Liverpool, once said that 'umpires do the job because of their lust for power'. Public fame or notoriety reminded people that umpires were incomparably the most powerful people on the cricket field.

In 1946 the bowler's end umpire in a game between Barbados and British Guiana had a fit of power madness, or absent-mindedness. He let the bowler, D.

144

F. Hill, bowl a fourteen ball over. There were no wides or no-balls. The game was using the 8 ball over commonly used in the West Indies and Australia, and the six extra balls were the result of the umpire miscounting. It might have passed quietly by, as miscounting has always been one of umpires' most common mistakes, but in this case the miscounting was both gargantuan and traumatic: the 14th ball dismissed Everton Weekes, the local idol, LBW. The umpire got away with his life.

England had tried the eight- instead of the six-ball over, in club cricket from 1938 and in first class cricket from 1939, but returned to the six-ball over in 1945. Overseas cricket was given official permission to go on using eight-ball overs.

Variation in the length of overs was one of several differences that developed on a national basis and was used as an argument against countries exchanging a few of their best umpires for a season. There was quite a bit of support for this idea in the early 1950s. Top English umpires like Chester and Lee could spend the winter in Australia and a couple of good Australian umpires could spend the summer in England. Both sides would then learn a lot about the other country's playing and umpiring techniques, manners and customs, which would make them more understanding when that side toured their country.

One fact militating against the exchange idea was that individual umpires had less financial reason to support it than before. In 1952 English first class umpires finally secured year-round pay: £5 a week and £5 a match, plus expenses. This improvement was designed to induce cricketers who were just giving up the game to become umpires instead of opening sports shops. The winter season became much less bleak when it was not so fraught with financial worries.

But the best excuse for not organising beneficial umpire exchanges was that in 1952 the Association of Cricket Umpires was formed, the aim of which was to improve the standard of umpiring at every level of cricket. Though its training courses and examinations were not intended to produce umpires at the first class level, it was felt that better umpiring all through cricket was bound to have a good effect on first class umpiring and, ultimately, help to improve international cricket relations, rendering an exchange system unnecessary.

In 1953 E. W. Swanton wrote: 'The club umpire is commonly portrayed as a somewhat decrepit individual, weary of eye and limb, and too often the portrait is more or less true to life.'

It was to put that situation right and to raise standards from the bottom up that the ACU came into existence and has been coaching umpires and would-be umpires ever since. Only the dedicated paid the fee and spared the time, usually in the form of evening classes, to become pupils of the ACU. Most club and village umpires were not in that category and even if they had been, few of them had a qualified teacher near them. Nevertheless, the ACU was a pillar of the centralised and conscientious post-war game; it was the first umpiring institution and the first official recognition that umpires were as important to the game as players. Eighteenth-century cricketers would have been amazed.

The ACU would not have survived if there had not been a wide general demand for its services. But obviously the strongest demand for good umpires was in international cricket. The home authorities gave the touring side a list of the umpires they proposed to use in the coming Test matches; if there were serious objections to any of them, he was removed from the list. Such requests were nearly always granted. It would have been as unpleasant for the umpires as for the players to have to persist in the face of an obvious breakdown in confidence.

After the first Australian Test at Brisbane in 1958, England asked that one of the umpires, Mel McInnes, should not be chosen again to umpire on the tour, and the request was turned down. But this was an exception to the rule. When the Australians were in England back in 1953 they had asked not to have Chester umpiring again after the Headingley Test. It was a bold request to make about the umpire widely agreed to be the best in the world, but the MCC granted it. They went further than that and gave Chester the rest of the season off.

1953 was a sad season for Chester. He had been playing to the crowd more in the last couple of years, but that was not what bothered the Australians. What bothered them was that he seemed to be becoming anti-Australian, to the point where his decisions were biased. Previously he had talked racing to the fielders of both sides when he was at square leg but now he stood grimly silent, turning down appeals in an Australian accent. In the Headingley test he gave two not outs, which were clearly wrong, in favour of the English: one when Reg Simpson was run out and one when Compton was caught in the slips. The Australian captain, Lindsay Hassett, made a furious complaint to the MCC, who explained that Chester was ill and removed him from duty.

The English expected the same level of co-operation from the Australian Board of Control when they complained about McInnes on the 1958–9 tour, but they did not get it. The tour was a tense one throughout. England had wiped the floor with Australia last time they met, but the main reason relations were becoming strained was that Australian umpires did nothing about what the English considered to be flagrant throwing by Australian bowlers.

County committees had managed to keep throwing out of English cricket since the turn of the century, and English umpires had never really developed a concerted policy on how to handle throwing, which they still regarded as a job for county committees and captains. They were handicapped by the lack of a good, clear definition of throwing. The sort of arbitrary, point-blank umpiring which Phillips had used to wipe out throwing at the turn of the century, though effective, was regarded as attention-seeking and trouble-making.

In the early 1950s England had very little trouble with throwing and what little there was concerned spinners, not fast bowlers; the best thing, it was thought, was to leave it alone and it would die down. Thus, on the first day of the 1951 South African tour of England, Frank Chester was told by Sir Pelham Warner, the President of the MCC, that he would get no support if he no-balled McCarthy, the South African fast bowler with a suspect action. No English umpire had ever called a visiting bowler and the MCC was keen to maintain its lofty ideal of cricket as a force for friendship among nations.

Now and again an English umpire did call someone for throwing, but never in Test matches and never with any statement of official support. In 1952, to the astonishment of everyone, Paddy Corrall no-balled the left-arm spinner Lock, playing for Surrey against Worcestershire at Worcester. Lock was no-balled again by a West Indian umpire in a Test in Jamaica two years later. It was only his faster ball that was suspicious and when he went to Australia and New Zealand in 1958, and saw a film of his action, he changed his action.

By this time, however, everyone was on edge about throwing, in England and abroad. So much so that in their 1958 pre-season meeting at Lord's, the English first class umpires were told to keep a special eye out for it.

Ian Meckiff, the Australian bowler, was suspected of throwing on the Australian tour of South Africa in 1957–8 but the umpires agreed between themselves to hush it up. On the English tour of Australia in 1958–9 Meckiff got away with it again but was strongly criticised by both English and Australian journalists, who also attacked three other suspect bowlers in the Australian squad for endangering the good name of Australian cricket.

England were soundly beaten in the series. All of their batsmen thought Meckiff threw, some of them to the extent that they developed a psychological blockage and could not play him. But they did not make trouble about it while they were in Australia, where the Board of Control had not been helpful over their umpiring complaint and was unlikely to be helpful over this. Also, the Australians had not complained about the bad pitches they encountered in England two years before; it seemed only fair to be as restrained as they had been. The English captain, Peter May therefore refrained from complaining and the Australian umpires, with no pressure on them, did not call anyone for throwing.

But when the English team got home, they lodged a vigorous protest with the MCC, who urged Bradman to help it solve the problem. He watched the 1959 and 1960 films and got the Australian state captains to get rid of all their suspect bowlers, whom he was now convinced were chuckers. Meckiff lasted until 1963, when umpire Colin Egar ended his career by no-balling him at Brisbane.

Cricket was an officially international game and though it had trouble arriving at an international code of standards and umpiring, it was working steadily towards one. Umpires were the men who put the laws into effect, so it was as important for all the major countries to have the same umpiring standards as it was for them to have the same laws.

In the spring of 1959, when the Australian tour was still fresh in everyone's minds, Tom Smith, the Honorary Secretary of the ACU, published an article called 'Throwing – The Umpire's View'. It asked that if the problem was to be left to umpires, people should at least realise how difficult it was. Neither wrist movement nor bent arm at delivery necessarily indicated a throw; camera shots, especially in slow motion, were misleading because they exaggerated the perspective and fore-shortening of deliveries. He suggested that the square leg umpire should be the one to watch the bowler's arm and should not be afraid to consult his colleague.

An umpire should be allowed to ask a captain to take a suspect bowler off and after the match he should make a report to the club about him. But the easiest way to eradicate throwing, Smith claimed, was for captains not to put on bowlers with suspect actions.

The summer of 1961 showed how effective action of this sort by captains could be; one can only guess what a relief it must have been for umpires. The Australians came to England with a team which did not include four suspect bowlers; there was no controversy in the Test matches.

English umpires had exercised their authority the year before, when the South Africans came to England. Griffin was repeatedly no-balled for throwing and for dragging his back foot. The 'drag' had become a bugbear and given rise to a series of rulings on how far forwards and sideways the back foot could be dragged. Griffin kept the bowler's end umpire busy calling him for dragging and the square leg umpire busy calling him for throwing.

He took advice on his bowling action and modified but weakened it and, in trying to recover his power that summer, was no-balled by umpires Lee, Langridge, Copson, Bartley, Parks, Elliott and Buller. It was the end of his career and a sad triumph of umpiring solidarity, for the first time penalising a foreign bowler in England.

No-balling for throwing has always been one of umpires' nastiest duties. It is difficult and, where a popular bowler is concerned, unpopular. When Buller no-balled Rhodes, the Derbyshire fast bowler and hero, at Chesterfield in June 1965, he had to have a police escort from the ground. But what umpires most dislike about no-balling a bowler is that it will probably ruin his career. No-one who has been a cricketer likes sending a player out of the game. Chester said he dreaded calling bowlers more than anything else, for that reason.

He would not have enjoyed the 1960 season. He was spared it because he died in 1957, only two years after he retired. It was as if he couldn't live without umpiring.

11

The Modern Game

Today's cricket is never as good as yesterday's. That is the first law of cricket nostalgia, a quality which abounds among writers, spectators and lovers of the game. Players are less given to it. They have a more practical outlook. Many of the changes in modern cricket which continue to distress cricket traditionalists have been accepted philosophically, often enthusiastically, by players. Umpires' reactions are harder to fathom. Umpires seldom make their feelings public.

Over the last twenty years umpires have had to adapt to an immense number of changes, almost amounting to a revolution. One-day and knock-out competitions, on Sundays as well as the other six days of the week; match sponsorship; the domination of English cricket by overseas players; players moving county, even country, to play for the highest bidder; the disappearance of the gentlemen and players distinction; the emergence of women's cricket as a serious branch of the game; World Series Cricket.

Being an umpire in the midst of all this, particularly with television playbacks of every decision, requires nerves of steel. Even so, it is less likely to get its practioner killed or maimed than it would have a couple of centuries ago. Certainly the shape of the game has changed, but there have been gains as well as losses.

League cricket continues its tradition of afternoon matches and neutral umpires. Clubs continue, for the most part, to provide their own umpires or borrow a friend who knows the game. Schools use teachers or unoccupied boys as umpires. Women's cricket, like

151

"I hope to goodness they haven't brought in any new rules since last season."

village cricket, goes stolidly on playing week-end afternoon matches with a succession of player-umpires, spectator-umpires and the kind of extras and hangers-on who attach themselves to every team and often end up umpiring and dishing out advice. In the teeth of contemporary changes and troubles, umpires maintain their inheritance of being unpredictable and always in the wrong.

Doomed to general condemnation though they are by the nature of their job, English umpires remain at the top of the international umpiring league. There are those who think international cricket is so different from every other kind of cricket that county experience is of little value to Test match umpires, but most people still respect the experienced, professional English umpires more than any others.

Abroad, especially in Australia and South Africa, ex-players don't want to umpire, partly because it would remind them how much they miss playing and partly because they know all too well how players, newspapers and television bully umpires. As I sit writing this, news has come through that two of the best umpires in South Africa, Denzil Bezuidenhout and Oswald Schoof, have decided to retire from first class cricket because they have been so fiercely criticised by both the captain of the South African team and the captain of the rebel Australian team on tour there. Clive Rice, the South African captain, said he thought play had evolved over the last ten years but umpiring had stood still. Umpires in the Transvaal retaliated by walking off in all the premier league games in the state and handing team captains a written statement deploring players' interference in umpiring.

A similarly critical climate prevails everywhere, but though English umpires' pay has risen recently, it is still substantially lower than players' pay and lower than that in most decently paid jobs. Better pay for umpires might compensate them for the stresses of their job. In South Africa white umpires in white games get only average pay. What Rice meant by his suggestion that the game has evolved is obscure, but he is probably right that umpiring has not developed to keep pace with the game: modern umpires are not as self-confident and resilient as modern players.

A further pressure, and the speciality of our age, is media pressure. In the last thirty years appeals have become significantly more intimidating, while the decisions they call forth are subjected to a formidable barrage of analysis and discussion. More often than not, playbacks show an umpire's decision to be right, but they hang over every game, making a cool head and a sharp eye vital. At Sydney, there is a giant playback screen which does, literally, hang over every decision the umpires make. Playbacks cannot show the position from which a ball was bowled, the angle at which it reached the crucial point with which the umpire was concerned, or the perspective he used in making his judgement. But an umpire who broods on wrong decisions or what appear to have been wrong decisions is bound to lose confidence and make himself even more susceptible to bullying.

It is not just the tone but also the extent of modern media coverage that persecutes umpires. After a day's play in a big game there is heavy pressure put on umpires by journalists to explain their decisions. It is part of a new media voyeurism. It is now assumed that the public has a right to know everything that might help to explain what happens on the field, from umpires' romantic troubles to their experience of the male menopause. Umpires in general maintain an admirable resistance to this pressure; even the few umpires who have written books about themselves, unlike the many players, have revealed only the bare cricketing minimum about themselves.

Umpires train themselves to brood as little as possible, but every umpire remembers his big mistakes. It is in the nature of the job that good umpiring is forgotten; it is bad umpiring that is remembered, by umpires themselves as well as by players and public.

From time to time, the umpire is relieved of responsibility for a doubtful decision by the batsman himself, who heads for the pavilion without waiting for the raised finger. This habit of 'walking' used to be considered the height of good sportsmanship, admired by players and welcomed by umpires. But only in the south of England. It has never been admired in the north, where it is scorned as a weak, southern habit giving unnecessary help to the opposition. Decisions are the umpires' job, not the players', and nothing should be done to help umpires towards any decision which might be against the team's interests.

The issue hardly arises any more because hardly anyone walks any more, at least in first class cricket. David Constant, a member of the present first class umpire's list, has no doubt at all that walking is a good thing and its passing into history is a loss to the first class game. He reckons that when he started umpiring in 1969, 90 per cent of cricketers walked; ten years later 90 per cent of cricketers did not walk.

Constant puts this state of affairs alongside aggressive appealing, talking umpires into decisions and talking batsmen out, as symptoms of modern gamesmanship, which he attributes to the big money involved in today's cricket.

Not everyone agrees with him. League cricket does not just despise walking, but the whole fair play ethos. Traditionally, the leagues have been the playground of cheerful cheats. Bill Lilley, a local hero in the Yorkshire League, was a wicket-keeper with a whole repertoire of dishonest techniques. He stuck a hairpin in the end of his boot and touched the base of the stumps with it, to knock the bails off. It is the umpires' job to stop cheating. If they do not, it is the cheats' good luck. There is nothing modern about this attitude and it owes nothing to financial pressure. It is a natural product of northern, and especially league, professionalism, which puts the onus squarely on the umpires to keep the game in order.

Elsewhere in cricket, opinion generally holds that ethical standards have declined over the last twenty years as financial pressure has increased. First class cricket is played for much bigger money than it was a generation ago, and it carries side benefits, such as deodorant adverts and love-life revelations in Sunday papers, which can amount to a fortune for successful players. Inevitably, this leaves less room for ethics, and less time for the leisurely, social side of cricket which has always been one of the great strengths and attractions of the village and club game.

The Oxford City team still meets before and after matches in the King's Arms, next to Wadham College, where it has met since time out of mind. Club umpires sometimes join the players for a drink after the game, though not as often as old faithful umpires like John Paddon would have liked. Meals are more of a problem; serious clubs exclude umpires from team meals, or at least make them sit on their own, so that they can't be accused of bias. The more high class and highly financed the cricket, the less relaxed its social arrangements. Nowadays first class players tend to go straight off at the end of a game to the next game or celebrity television appearance and there is less friendly eating and drinking together, more tension and bad temper.

David Constant rates being asked for a drink as the highest praise an umpire can get. It means his decisions are not going to be endlessly criticised and that he has been accepted, at least for that evening, as one of the gang. Constant, like every first class umpire, misses playing cricket and takes a romantic view of its social life. All the more so because he stopped playing cricket when he was only twenty-seven, realising he would never make the grade as a county player. He is nostalgic for the more gentle and restrained cricket which he remembers as being still in existence in the late 60s and early 70s. Umpires do not see much of the frivolous side of cricket but they like to believe that it still exists. Constant is inclined to think that it has gone from first class cricket altogether and can now only be found in the village and club game.

Certainly tempers seem to snap more easily than they used to. Or perhaps it's just that they attract more attention when they do snap. Among the instructions to each umpire at the end of the present code of laws is a mention of his duty to report any player 'criticising his decisions by word or action, or showing dissent, or generally behaving in a manner which might bring the game into disrepute'. The report should be made to the other umpire and to the player's captain. If the captain proves ineffective in disciplining the offender, the umpire should then report him to the body in charge of the match. This is a long, tiring procedure to go through, involving a player the umpire is sure to meet again in another game, and he has to feel seriously aggrieved before he undertakes it.

In 1973, for the first time in a Test match, an umpire felt angry enough with a player to refuse to go on. Arthur Fagg was so indignant at the way the West Indian captain Rohan Kanhai swore and gesticulated at one of his decisions on the third day of the Edgbaston Test that he said he would not come out again the next day. What is more, he took the uncharacteristic step of telling a couple of journalists the reasons for his withdrawal.

If they will not accept decisions, there is no point carrying on. Why should I? I am nearly 60. I don't have to live with this kind of pressure. I've had to live with it for 2½ hours out there. People don't realise how bad it has become. I don't enjoy umpiring Tests any more . . . There is so much at stake . . . the game has changed, and not for the better. Umpires are under terrific pressure.

It took powerful persuasion by Dicky Bird, the other umpire, and by the team managers and ground officials to make him change his mind, and he would only do so after the West Indian team manager had apologised formally for Kanhai's behaviour. Even then, Fagg only came out after a substitute umpire had been found and had stood in for him for the first over. The West Indians put on a grim performance that morning. They bowled bouncers, ran down the pitch and slowed up the over rate until Fagg and Bird consulted about what, if anything, they should do about it.

They called both captains into their dressing-room during the lunch break and warned them that the game might have to be called off, or the fast bowlers taken off, unless the over rate speeded up and the bowling became less intimidating. It was the first ever instance of an umpires' off-the-field action group, and it was successful.

There is still a strong conservative lobby which disapproves of bullying umpires and seizes on incidents like the Kanhai one to press for tougher action against offenders. The trouble is that tougher action is usually left to the umpires to undertake because successful cricketers nowadays can afford to behave like prima donnas; if their counties take action against them, another county will snap them up. Tougher laws would only worsen the legal congestion of modern cricket.

Just occasionally umpires are lucky and do get active official support in dealing with trouble. In 1974, the year after the Kanhai incident, Geoff Arnold of Surrey became the first player in modern first class cricket to be suspended from playing for abusing an umpire. Peter Wight signalled one of Arnold's deliveries a wide, Arnold swore at him and the Test and County Cricket Board enforced a short disciplinary suspension. *The Times* commented with melancholy satisfaction: 'Swearing at an umpire is still, mercifully, a good enough reason for a cricketer to be censured, as it is even in football.'

The day after that, 9 August 1974, Glamorgan suspended an all-rounder, Michael Llewellyn, 'who was sent off by the umpires during a second XI match at Pontypridd this week for allegedly refusing his captain's request to field at short leg'.

That kind of support, from the TCCB and from individual counties, is all too rare, and it is easy to understand why. Part of cricket's character, despite plenty of vigorous exceptions, is its unwritten code of behaviour. Attempting to define and enforce that code legally would undermine the game's informal charm.

Cricket has only had a fixed constitution and governing body since 1969, arguably because it has only needed one since then. The TCCB, as its name suggests, is responsible for the administration of Test and county cricket, and tries to maintain cricket tradition by keeping a low profile. It is part of the Cricket Council, which also includes the MCC and the National Cricket Association, the guardian of humble cricket. In effect, the Cricket Council is British cricket's government, and is appropriately reticent. No-one, least of all umpires, would want the Cricket Council taking part in the day-to-day management of cricket.

Requests for help in solving difficult umpiring problems are regularly sent to the TCCB and the MCC, from all levels of cricket, but the council takes the initiative in dealing with problems only very occasionally, when all else has failed. Where umpires are concerned, it steps in to confirm, not supersede, their authority. In April 1971, after the Australasian tour, which had given rise to serious trouble over umpires' decisions, the Council issued one of its rare statements:

> The Cricket Council, as the governing body of cricket in the U.K., must record their grave concern about incidents involving dissent from umpires' decisions, whether by word or deed. . . . In dealing with such breaches of discipline the Council and the TCCB, through their Disciplinary Committee, will not hesitate to use their wide powers which include the termination of the registration of a player.

The thinking behind this is clear: however bad the umpiring, its authority must be upheld. As with umpires, so with the governing force behind them, it is usually enough, as it was in this case, to show sharp teeth.

Dicky Bird is an extrovert, ideal for the job of extending umpiring powers as far as they will go and spelling them out, as he did over the trouble between Kanhai and Arthur Fagg. Fagg, who has since died, was a quiet umpire in the 'Bob' Thoms tradition. Bird is a character umpire in the Caldecourt and Skelding tradition. His white cap is his trademark, just as Caldecourt's Napoleonic hat was his trademark.

But even Bird, who thrives on emergencies, finds the tension generated by modern crowds too much of a good thing. He thinks chants, such as the 'Kill Kill Kill' which used to accompany Procter's bowling in South Africa, are bad for cricket. Like the Dennis Lillee style of cut-throat appealing, they exhaust and annoy umpires, making them less likely to give appeals their proper attention.

Modern crowds may well be less violent and less soaked in drink than eighteenth-century crowds, but they are definitely more violent, abusive, aggressive and drunk than crowds twenty years ago. In 1980 David Constant was the victim of a physical attack by a man angered that the Cornhill Centenary Test was taking so long to restart after rain. Even Bird sometimes feels nervous in front of modern crowds.

All umpires have a horror of crowd trouble, which

159

they are pretty well powerless to prevent and completely powerless to control. All umpires think crowd behaviour has worsened over the last twenty years. Whether this is partly as a result of the example set by one day cricket with its large, impatient and often beer-sodden crowds, is beside the point. The fact is that coping with crowd invasions, getting the equipment safely off the ground, is one of the talents all modern umpires in first class cricket must try to develop.

Crowd trouble is the main reason umpires dislike having to take teams off the field for bad light. Even now that they are armed with light meters, which give an appearance of technical reasoning to back up their decisions, umpires are dogged by ill feeling over bad light decisions. Players and spectators are sceptical about light meters, which do not cater for random clouds and do not inspire confidence. Most umpires keep their opinions on light meters to themselves.

Bird likes light meters because they represent some sort of visible support for umpires. Gadgets suit Bird. He is a professional personality and was voted Yorkshire Personality of the Year in 1977, which shows not only how important cricket still is in Yorkshire but how honoured a status well-known modern umpires can reach nowadays.

As umpires' responsibilities in the game continue to increase, so their part in the game gets more noticeable, even though most of them try to stay as inconspicuous as possible. Constant takes the quick, quiet line if he sees close fielders trying to talk a batsman out; he tells them to cut it out at once. Most league, club and village umpires regard the talking tactic as a fair part of the rough and tumble of cricket, and leave it alone unless it becomes too gross a piece of gamesmanship. A feel for the particular circumstances and customs of each game is one of an umpire's most valuable tools.

Odd and unusual duties, even if they are unpleasant, can make for light relief. When an IRA bomb scare interrupted the Lord's Test in 1973, Bird sat on the covers, guarding the pitch and talking and joking with his public. In one of the 1974 Tests against the Indians, Gavaskar's hair kept getting in his eyes while he was batting and he asked Bird to cut it for him. Bird reached into his pocket, pulled out a pair of scissors and had a fine time recording the first known instance of 'hair cutting stopped play.'

All umpires carry emergency supplies, but Bird's cater for a more exotic range of emergencies than most: scissors, penknife, gum, needle and cotton, safety pins, rag, spare ball and bail, light meter and six small red barrels, given him by a brewery company, to count the balls in each over.

Oddities still crop up in first class cricket, thank God. In the hot summer of 1975 a streaker 'outraged public decency' in the Lord's Test when the temperature was 93°. That same summer snow stopped play in a county match at Buxton.

But English oddities, such as gratuitous nakedness, pale into insignificance next to some of the acts of God in cricket abroad, especially in India and Pakistan. Play at Lahore was stopped by an earthquake in 1937–8 and at Poona by a deranged monkey in 1951–2. By comparison, the parachutists who interrupted the 1974 match between Nottinghamshire and India at Trent Bridge by inadvertently falling short of their target and landing near the pitch, constituted a mere side-show.

Now that there are so many one-day matches, anything that breaks an umpire's concentration is as much a trial as a relaxation. The first knock-out competition took place in 1963. Today there are a wealth of different knock-out, one-day, limited-over matches, each with a different total number of overs and a different number allowed to each player. Remembering what the rules are for each game has become a big part of an umpire's job.

Enforcing the rules is not always the carnival job it can be in the early rounds of knock-out competitions. The physical and mental pressure in one-day matches is unremitting. In 1971 the semi-final of the Gillette Cup was nicknamed the Lamplight Match because it did not finish until 8.50 p.m., with the pavilion lights shining through the darkness at Old Trafford. The umpires had been standing since 11.00 in the morning.

One-day cricket is far more popular than three-day cricket, at which crowds have been declining steadily since the 1950s. The disadvantages of this change are obvious, but so are the advantages. Even though the playing season is still pretty much of a write-off for home life, every umpire dislikes the protracted hotel living to which three-day games condemn him. A one-day, one-night stay is less disruptive for his family than a three-day, three-night stay.

Village and club cricket has always been a one-day affair and its umpiring has always been less formal and more variable than that of first class cricket. But even village and club cricket sometimes gets commercial sponsorship nowadays, which brings publicity and extra tension in its wake. Despite these pressures, the National Club Knock-Out, founded in 1969, and the National Village Championship, founded in 1972, have been huge successes, with good, easy relations between players, crowds and umpires, who in the early stages of the contests are local men.

From the umpires' point of view, sponsorship tends to make the public more demanding, but as far as the sponsors are concerned, it makes the umpires a success whatever they do. For sponsors, all publicity is good publicity, and controversy is the best publicity of all.

The growth of one-day cricket puts a subtle strain on umpires. Many find the adjustments necessary between one-day and other matches a strain. Three- and five-day cricket requires an umpire to keep up his concentration even when there seems to be nothing much happening; its climaxes creep rather than charge up on participants. In 1974, for example, when one-day cricket had begun its shake-up of English cricket, the umpires of the Test against Australia at Old Trafford had to switch back to their slowest of slow gears to last through Simpson's 12 hours 40 minutes at the crease, the longest innings Englishmen had ever endured. He went on to make 311 and Australia went on batting until an hour into the third day, when Simpson declared at 656 for 8. Worse was to come. Barrington took 11½ hours to accumulate 256 out of England's total of 611, the only time a Test team has ever made over 600 in response to an innings of 600 or more. England were still playing their first innings on the fifth day.

Vexed questions such as exactly what constitutes time-wasting, need different factors to be taken into account in one-day matches and longer matches, and altogether different ones when a Simpson is trudging it out with a Barrington at a maximum run-rate of 20 an hour. David Evans, the recently retired Test umpire, whiled away the time in slow matches by working out the astrological signs of the players, according to what he saw as their personality characteristics. But he would rather have been kept busy. Time-wasting is one of those 'fair and unfair play' questions which has no written definition and can only be resolved by the umpire's judgement. Short-pitched bowling is another one. Both are unpopular issues with umpires.

In the 1965 Leeds Test, Griffith, the West Indian fast bowler, bowled a bouncer to Graveney. Despite Graveney being a good batsman high in the batting order, umpires Elliott and Buller conferred and Elliott told Griffith that if he bowled another one, he would be no-balled. Such rapid action would be unthinkable today. We have got used to bouncers, which some people

163

regard as a legitimate part of a fast bowler's armoury, except when used to excess against tail-enders.

In 1976 at Manchester, Close and Edrich were subjected to a barrage of short-pitched bowling from the West Indians, which the umpires did very little to stop. Presumably they thought Close and Edrich good enough batsmen to be safe from physical danger. Close was professionally immune to intimidation and stood without flinching while balls bounced off his body. Edrich said he was so angry and frightened he nearly walked off. 'Surely cricket hasn't come to this?' he said later.

That same year the International Cricket Conference, the nearest cricket gets to a world governing body, put bouncers at the top of its list of concerns and emerged with the earth-shattering conclusion that it was up to umpires to decide when bouncers were unacceptable, always bearing in mind that bowling bouncers to tail-enders in any circumstances was hardly cricket. Club umpires have a simpler time of it because they encounter fewer bouncers. The lower down the scale of cricket, the lower is players' tolerance of bouncers: if they appear in village cricket, it is to the accompaniment of equally short-pitched remarks.

The legitimacy of bouncers was one of the many issues on which Kerry Packer's World Series Cricket differed from the ICC. Packer regarded bouncers, in any number, at any batsmen, as a reasonable part of his modern, macho cricket. Most things in Packer's game were in deliberately bad cricket taste, to shock cricket out of its complacent conservatism. But he offered jobs as performing showmen, supported by cartoons and mock sound effects, to two English umpires, Constant and Bird, straight out of the complacent conservative circuit, for the simple reason that he thought they were the best umpires in the world.

They both refused his offer. It had been bad enough for cricket traditionalists when English umpires abandoned their knee-length white coats in favour of the short, Australian style of coat in 1969. But at least the manner within the coats remained classically under-

*"You're going to ruin a perfectly good
cricket match, damage the good name of
umpires everywhere, and do precisely
nothing to improve race relations."*

stated and the short coats quickly became a tradition
themselves.

Constant, who is a campaigner for umpires to be paid
the same as players, refused Packer's offer because it
was too small. It was £8,000 for a short winter season,
and though that is more than an umpire would get for
the same period of time in ordinary cricket, it was half
as much as Packer's players were getting.

Bird refused for more traditional reasons. As he said
in his press statement, 'I don't wish to take any action
which would be prejudicial to my position as an umpire
in Test and County Cricket.'

The fact remains that the most obvious reason village
and small club cricket is so much more relaxed than first

class cricket is that money does not enter into it. It can afford to be more light-hearted about its misdemeanours and eccentricities. A. A. Milne used to bowl from behind and over the heads of the umpires, causing the umpires great amusement and problems about when to count unusual bowling as dangerous bowling.

Leg spin has become so rare in first class cricket that it almost counts as dangerous bowling just because of its surprise value. But the village cricket leg spinner, often an elder statesman of the side, still survives in places and still gets impossible LBW decisions from village umpires.

Women's cricket is a more unexpected home of leg spin and of umpires familiar enough with it to know what to watch for when it is bowled. There are many women's cricket clubs now and a lot of them boast young members leg spinning and googlying their way through the game. There are few officially-qualified women umpires, however, and women's small club teams usually play, like village teams, with a series of team members standing as umpires and being relieved by someone else when a wicket falls and they have to get ready to bat. The standard of umpiring is as variable as it is in men's small club cricket.

Women's umpires are usually female except in the first-class game, where they are always female. The day has only just dawned when men's first class cricket has, at last, accepted a female umpire. Recently Pat Carrick stood in a Shell Trophy game between Canterbury and Wellington, to the outspoken dismay of Richard Hadlee, who still questions a woman's place in a man's environment, where she might be subjected to verbal abuse and worse. Such arguments of course are those of tradition and prejudice. They do, however, have some basis in the facts of cricketing life. Occasionally a men's club or village team employs a woman as umpire, and she needs to be tough to withstand the jibes and insults she receives.

The sex war is hard fought in cricket. Whereas women play equally happily with male or female umpires, men are inclined to get so resentful when confronted with a female umpire that they unleash dreadful, furious strokes and get themselves out, which makes them even more resentful. Men, especially small men with moustaches, are particularly bad at accepting an unfavourable decision from a member of the opposite sex. The few men's club matches I have umpired have been an ordeal.

Cricket in New Caledonia, on the other hand, makes more flippant use of the sex war. The game is played on Sundays by women; the umpires, to be neutral, must be men. They lean on bats and decide between them who has won when everyone is too tired to go on. There is no fixed time limit to the game. The players wear straw hats and fit frangipani flowers over their ears. Older women employ younger women to run for them and to influence the umpires' decisions.

Cold weather and a long cricketing heritage has prevented such seductions from winning over the English game. English umpires, even at the humblest level of cricket, are determinedly resistant to attempts to influence them. A keen umpire would rather turn down invitations to the pub and be reckoned stand-offish than drink with players and risk accusations of bias. Even friendly chatter with players has to stop short of making the umpire one of the lads, lest it becomes difficult for him to exercise his authority. David Constant makes a point of standing in one or two village matches every April, before the first class season begins, to get into practice, especially at striking the right balance between serious objectivity and friendly cheerfulness.

It is ironic that in an age when cricket has never been so conscientious about its umpires, training and laws, Constant got his job, like Bird, simply by writing to the MCC and asking for it, without examination, interview or previous experience. For the most part, though, English umpiring has succumbed to modern seriousness.

First class umpires have a medical every April, to check their eyes, ears and blood pressure. Nowadays only amateur and village cricket is willing to tolerate the deaf, blind, idiotic and partisan umpire who is as old as the pavilion.

Amateur umpires still lend charm, if not expertise, to Indian first class cricket, where there is a tradition of keen, wildly erratic and ambitious amateur umpiring. Mr. P. N. Polishwalla's pamphlet 'All About Umpiring', privately produced and printed in 1917, was an early item in the proud flow of amateur umpiring literature which still pours off private presses in old-fashioned, affluent Indian houses where the Empire is missed and the shelves are lined with old Wisdens.

It is not like that in the higher echelons of English cricket. Here umpires are more closely identified than ever before with the cricket establishment. E. J. Smith played for Warwickshire from 1904 to 1930, then became a coach at Edgbaston and President of the Midland Counties Umpires Association, which supplies well-trained umpires for league and friendly matches. He remained in those jobs until the 60s, and right up until his death in 1979 was a familiar figure to everyone who loved Warwickshire cricket, a pillar of the club establishment.

First class umpires now advise first class selectors, officially and unofficially. But this close identification with the establishment has its disadvantages. In 1964–5 when Australia toured the West Indies, a local umpiring dispute left the Georgetown Test without an umpire. Gomez, a former West Indian all-rounder and a selector, stepped in and umpired, running off at close of play to do the radio summary. The Australians complained that as Gomez had been one of those who selected Griffith, the fast bowler, he was obviously not going to no-ball him. They thought Griffith a suspect thrower and wanted another umpire who would take a dispassionate view of the matter.

At the other end of the scale, village cricket, despite all the changes it has undergone in the last twenty years, is still played and umpired for pleasure and still exposes umpires to harassment, hatred and humour. Umpiring is a serious business and also a funny business. In an ideal world, umpires, like policemen and traffic wardens, would not exist. But in the actual world, which cricket continues to try to make as ideal and delightful as possible, umpires have made an honourable place for themselves. As E. B. V. Christian wrote in 'At the Sign of the Wicket',

> Shall I never storm or swear
> Just because the umpire's fair? . . .
> If he will not favour me,
> What care I how fair he be?

Index

Aborigines, 106
accidents, 33–4, 102
Addington, 38
Adelaide, 129
Albemarle, Duke of, 63
All-Englanders, 87
Alton, 86
Anne, Queen, 23
appeals, 114–15, 140–1, 153–4
Arbroath, 98
Arnold, Geoff, 158
Artillery Ground, Finsbury, 24, 37–8, 39, 42
Association of Cricket Umpires (ACU), 15, 16, 145–6
Austen, William, 46
Australia, cricket in, 97–8, 106–7, in England, 106 (1878), 137 (1948), 146–7 (1953), 149 (1961), 163 (1974) in South Africa, 148 (1957–8) in West Indies, 168 (1964–5) umpiring in, 127, 129–30, 145–7, 153
Australian Board of Control, 147, 148–9
Aylesbury, 81
Aylward, James, 54

bad light, 160
Bagshaw, Harry, 123
bails, 32, 51
Bainbridge, H. W., 119
balls, 30, 138–9
Banister, Mr, 88
Barbados, 144–5
Barker, Tom, 99
Barnes, Christopher, 83
Barnes, S. F., 125
Barnsley, 125

Barrington, K., 163
Bartley, 150
bats, 30, 53–4, 59, 97
batting, 53, 70
Bayley, John, 80–1, 93
Beadster, William, 57
Beauclerk, Rev Lord Frederick, 72
Bedford, Rev W. K. R., 32
Beecroft, Mr, 86
Beldham, Billy, 58, 59, 84–5, 119
Bell's Life, 81–2, 86
Bentinck, Lord, 69
Bentley, Henry, 72, 75
Bentley, John, 72
Berkshire, 40, 56–7
Berlemont, Gaston, 118–19
betting, 20, 23, 26, 44, 47, 57, 84–6, 95
Bezuidenhout, Denzil, 153
Biggleswade, 91
Bird, H. D. ('Dicky'), 157, 159, 160–1, 164, 165, 167
Birmingham, 115
Birmingham and District Cricket Association, 105
Birmingham and District League, 105, 118
Bishop Wearmouth, 77
Bligh, Hon E., 69
Bolton, Duke of, 64
bookies, 47, 84–5
Bootle, 131
Boots, John, 33
Boult family, 58
boundaries, 31, 70, 104
Bournemouth, 109
bowling, 29, 49, 52–3
bodyline, 129–30
bouncers, 163–4
leg spin, 141, 166

over-arm, 73, 77, 78–82, 110–11
rolling, 29, 30
round-arm, 66, 67–75, 77, 81, 82,
   90, 111, 121–2
seam, 139
short-pitched, 163–4
swerve, 139
swing, 132–3, 139
throwing, 64, 110–14, 136,
   147–50
under-arm, 30, 52–3, 64, 67, 71–2,
   74, 111
Boxall, Tom, 53
Boxgrove, 18
Bradford Challengers, 90
Bradford League, 118
Bradman, Sir Donald, 129, 130, 131,
   137, 139, 149
Bray, 58
Brechin, 98, 100
Brechin Advertiser, 98
bribery, 40, 84–5, 87
Brighton, 51, 89
Brisbane, 146, 149
British Guiana, 144–5
Broadbridge, Jem, 73, 74, 75
Broadhalfpenny Down, 56, 61, 62–3
Brodrick, Mr, 25–32
Brooking, G. A., 131
Brown, F. R., 134
Buckinghamshire, 40–2
Budd, E. H., 70
Buller, Sid, 9–10, 150, 163
Bunbury, Mr, 55
Burghfield, 56–7
Burke, Perry, 137–8
Burley, 102
Bury and Norwich Post, 75
Buxton, 161

Caldecourt, William, 74, 77–80, 82,
   93, 95, 98, 114, 126, 159
Camber, 95
Cambridge Chronicle, 81
Cambridge Union, 81
Cambridge University Womens'
   Cricket Club, 12–13
Canada, 106
Canterbury, 166
Carrick, Pat, 166
catches, 35, 60–1
Charles II, King, 25, 72
Charlton, Sussex, 37

Chelmsford Chronicle, 84
Chelsea, 34
Cheltenham, 104, 128
Cheltenham Ladies' College, 12
Chester, Frank, 124, 128–31, 134,
   137, 140–8, 150
Chesterfield, 150
Chichester, 18
Chilgrove, 37
Christian, E. B. V., 169
Church of England, 94
Clapham Common, 20, 34
Clarke, William, 87, 92
class differences, 96–7, 143–4
Clerkenwell, 19
Close, Brian, 164
clothing, 35, 58, 89–90, 101, 116–17,
   164–5
Collins, W. E. W., 121–2, 124
Compton, Dennis, 147
Constant, David, 154–5, 156, 159,
   160, 164–5, 167
Coote, Cyril, 13
Copson, 150
Cornhill Centenary Test, 159
Corrall, Paddy, 148
Cotswolds, 140
country house cricket, 105–6, 124
county cricket, 124–5, 138
County Cricket Council, 106
Coventry, 34, 55
Coventry Mercury, 55
Cowell's Athletic Association, 117
Coxheath, 20
Cricket Council, 158–9
Cricket magazine, 111, 123
crowd behaviour, 28, 33–4, 37–8,
   54, 61, 97–8, 117, 159–60
Cumberland, Captain, 69

Dalton, 86, 90
Dark, 82
Darlington, 77
Davies, Dai, 144
Day, Daniel, 90
dead balls, 45, 116–17
Dean, Jimmy, 104
Dearman, John, 81–2
Denis, 88
Denison, William, 78–9
Denton, 81–2
Deptford Unity, 99
Derbyshire, 89, 150

Dexter, Ted, 9
Dorset, Duke of, 27, 54, 63, 64
drink, and cricket, 19, 43, 63, 92, 95

Edgbaston, 157, 168
Edrich, John, 164
Egar, Colin, 149
Elliott, Charlie, 150, 163
Ellis, 39
Ellis, C. H., 102
Emmett, Tom, 102
Endean, Russell, 144
England, team, 42, 50, 51, 54–5, 60,
 63, 68, 71, 80, 85–7, passim
English Illustrated Magazine, 32
Essex, 115, 119
Eton, 45
Evans, David, 163
Evening Standard, 137

Fagg, Arthur, 156–7, 159
Fairfax, 98
Farr, Charles, 99
Farrar, Dean, 94–5
fielding, 61
Fiji Islands, 97
Finsbury, 24, 37–8
First World War, 124
follow-on, 91, 116
Forest Ground, Nottingham, 74
Forest Hill Cricket Club, 109
Frederick, Prince of Wales, 25, 37,
 38–9, 42
Free Foresters, 101
Fry, C. B., 113

Gage, Sir William, 25
Gale, F., 100–1
gambling, 20, 23, 26, 44, 47, 57,
 84–6, 95
Gavaskar, S. M., 161
Gentleman's Magazine, 47
Gentlemen v Players, 96, 143–4
The George Hotel, Henfield, 127
Georgetown, 168
Gibb, Paul, 142–3
Gillette Cup, 161–2
Glamorgan, 158
Gloucester City, 136
Gloucestershire, 133
Glover, A. C., 115
gloves, 90
Godalming, 89

Goddard, Tom, 133
Goldwin, William, 21–2
Gomez, G. E., 168
Good, Bartholomew, 78
Goodwood, 26, 29, 73
Gosseltine, George, 71
Grace, E. M., 100
Grace, G. F., 116–17
Grace, W. G., 94, 96–7, 98, 100,
 102–4, 108, 111, 112, 114–15
Graveney, Tom, 163
Green Man and Still, 84–5
Griffin, G., 150
Griffith, Charlie, 163, 168
Grimston, Hon Robert, 91
Grub Street Journal, 34
Gwynn, Nell, 72

Hadlee, Richard, 166
Halifax Clarence Club, 86
Hall, Harry, 53
Halnaker, 42
Hambledon, 21, 49–51, 53–4, 55–6,
 58, 59, 61, 62–4, 68
Hammond, Wally, 137
Hampshire, 22, 51
handled the ball, 44
Harris, David, 52, 53
Harris, Lord, 97–8, 111
Harting, 56
Hartley, Squire, 46
Hassett, Lindsay, 147
Hastings, 118
Hatfield, 86
hats, 89–90
Hayes, Richard, 51, 52
Haygarth, A., 108
Headingley, 146–7
Hendon, Sunderland, 77
Henfield, 24, 33, 79, 127
Herefordshire, 104–5
Hertfordshire County Press, 86
Heygate, R. B., 126
Hill, D. F., 144–5
hit the ball twice, 44–5
hit wicket, 44
Hobbs, Sir Jack, 125, 141–2
Hodson, 78
hopping, 72
Hove, 102
Huddersfield, 90
Huddersfield League, 118
Humphreys, Mr, 79

Hunt, Tom, 92–3
Hutton, Sir Leonard, 143, 144

India, 109, 129, 139–40, 160–1, 168
injuries, 33–4, 102
Instructions to Umpires, 108–9
International Cricket Conference, 130, 164
Ipswich, 117
IRA, 160
Ireland, 124
Islington, 43

Jamaica, 148
Japan, 104
Jardine, 130
Jenner-Fust, Mr H., 45
Jessop, Gilbert, 118
Jones, Ernest, 113
Jones, Rev., 121

Kanhai, Rohan, 157, 159
Kathiawar, 139–40
Keeble, G., 96
Kennington Common, 33
Kent, 22, 25, 35, 36, 38, 42, 43, 50–1, 61, 68, 72, 106, 115, 125
Kentish Gazette, 52
Kirkham, 88
Knaresborough, 92–3
Knight, G. T., 73–4
Knighton, 117
Knole Park, 25

Lady's Magazine, The, 71
Lahore, 161
Lambert, William, 69, 85
Lambourn, 52
Lancashire, 111, 112, 114, 138
Lancashire League, 118
Lanc, James, 83
Lanc, John, 83
Lane *v* Barnes, 83, 84
Langridge, 134, 150
Languard Fort, 117
Larwood, 129–30
Lau Islands, 97
lawn mowers, 90, 100
laws, 36, 42–6, 50, 51, 57, 59–60, 62, 67–76, 107, 116, 120–1
Lazenby, 98
LBW (leg before wicket), 45, 59–60, 81–3, 119–21, 131–2, 141

league cricket, 110, 118, 138, 151, 155
Lee, Frank, 130, 141–2, 145, 150
Leeds, 163
Leer, 'Little George', 63
leg-byes, 91, 134
leg play, 45, 119–21
Leicester, 34, 55
Leicester, John Sidney, Earl of, 25
Leicester East End, 117
Leighton Buzzard, 81
Lennox, Col, 69
Lennox, Duke of, 63
Lewes, 102
Leyton, 143
Lillee, Dennis, 159
Lilley, Bill, 155
Lilly, 96
Lillywhite, John, 80, 111, 114
Lillywhite, William, 73, 74–6, 80
Lisson Grove, 67, 72
Littleborough, 118
Llewellyn, Michael, 158
Lock, G. A. R., 148
London, 22, 24, 36–42, 46–8, 50
London Club, 37, 38, 42
London Magazine, The, 37–8, 58
Lord, Thomas, 36, 65, 67, 70
Lord's, 51, 56, 65, 67, 72, 75, 78–80, 84, 85, 90, 92, 93, 100–1, 103–4, 116, 134, 141–2, 143, 160–1
lost ball, 117
Luff, A., 96
Lyttleton, Hon R. H., 121

McCarthy, C. N., 148
McInnes, Mel, 146–7
MacLaren, A. C., 113
Maidenhead, 57–8
Maidstone, 18
Manchester, 164
Mann, Sir Horace, 27, 54, 55–6
Markham, Captain, 69
Marlborough College, 94
Marsden, Tom, 74
Martin, Richard, 18
Marylebone Cricket Club (MCC), 36, 43, 60, 65, 66–7, 69–70, 71–6, 77–82, 91, 99, 103, 107, 108–9, 110, 112, 116, 120, 130, 147, 148, 149, 158, 167
Matthews, 75
May, Peter, 149

173

Meadows Ground, Nottingham, 65
Meckiff, Ian, 148–9
media, 153–4
Melbourne, 129
Melville, 133
Middlesex, 40–2, 51, 98–9
Midland Counties Umpires
  Association, 168
Mikes, George, 137
Miller, Keith, 137
Milne, A. A., 166
Minor Counties Association, 110
Minor Counties Championship, 125
minor counties cricket, 110
Mitcham, 24, 33, 38, 46–7, 80–1
Mitchell, R. A. H., 100
Mitford, Mary Russell, 71
Mold, Arthur, 112, 113–14
Monson, Hon G., 69
Morning Herald, 71
Morning Post, The, 54
Mousley, 38–9
Moulsey Hurst, 38–9, 50, 60
Murray, John, 9
Mycroft, Tom, 115
Mynn, Alfred, 82, 83, 89, 92, 110

National Club Knock-Out, 162
National Cricket Association, 158
National Village Championship,
  162
Needham, Mr, 55
New Caledonia, 167
New South Wales, 107, 130
New York, 107
New Zealand, 129
Newick, 33
Nimbalkar, B. B., 139–40
nips, 45
no-balls, 44, 69, 79, 150
North Staffordshire League, 118
notches, 22, 30–1, 62
Nottingham, 65, 69, 74, 85, 88, 91,
  92, 103
Nottingham Review, 74, 92
Nottinghamshire, 10, 87, 103, 111,
  112, 161
Nyren, John, 21, 49–53, 55, 59–60,
  61, 62–4, 66, 67, 69, 119
Nyren, Richard, 27, 52, 64

obstruction, 45, 96, 100, 144
Old Trafford, 114, 162, 163

Oldner, George, 47
one-day matches, 20, 28–9, 160,
  161–3
Osbaldeston, Squire, 70
Oval, 80, 90, 92, 111, 144
overs, 110, 145
Owen, Canon Robert, 89
Oxford City, 136, 155
Oxford University Womens' Cricket
  Club, 10–11, 13

Packer, Kerry, 164–5
Paddon, John, 136, 143, 155
pads, 90
Pakistan, 161
Parks, 150
Parr, George, 87
Parry, 133
patronage, 24–8, 38–9, 54
Pavri, M. E., 109
payments, 39–40, 127–8, 145, 153,
  165
Payne, James, 140–1
Paynter, Eddie, 142
Penenden, 68
Penshurst, 25, 35
Pepperharrow, 25
Peregrine, Tom, 122
Pfeiffer, Knowles, 125
Philadelphia, 106, 107
Phillips, Jim, 113–14, 147
Pilch, Fuller, 83, 92, 95
pitches, 29–30, 40, 70, 90, 100–1,
  132
Platts, 116–17
Polishwalla, P. N., 168
Pontypridd, 158
Poona, 139–40, 161
popping crease, 31–2
Portman family, 67
Post Boy, The, 20
Postman, The, 20
Powlett, Rev Charles, 64
Preston, 88
Preston Chronicle, 88
Prince's Ground, 115
prizes, 87
procter, 159
protective clothing, 73, 90
pubs, 43
Pycroft, Rev J., 75, 90, 93, 94

'Quid', 95, 99, 107

174

Radley, 121
The Ram, Smithfield, 19
Reading, 40
Reading Mercury, 56
Reeves, Bill, 130–1, 132, 134
Reigate, 53, 88
Rhodes, A. E. G., 150
Rice, Clive, 153
Rich, David, 100
Richmond, 28, 47–8, 88
Richmond, Duke of, 25–32, 35, 40, 42, 73
Ring, Mr, 59
Rochdale, 81–2
Rogate, 56
Roses matches, 134, 138
Row, Mr, 34
Rowan, Athol, 144
Royton, 118
Rugby, 102
rules *see* laws
run outs, 32–3
runs, 30–1, 62
Russell, 115
Ryle, J. C., 75

Sackville, Lord John, 25
Sackville family, 25
Saffron Walden, 81
St Austell Club, 75–6
St John's Wood, 67
Schoof, Oswald, 153
score-cards, 44, 69
scorers, 31, 44, 92, 93
Scores and Biographies, 80, 90, 108
Sefton, 131
Sevenoaks, 51
Shaw, Alfred, 103
Sheffield, 33, 74, 88
Sheffield Mercury, 88
Shell Trophy, 166
Shepherd's Bush Cricket Club, 140–1
Sheppard, David, 144
Sherwood Forest Cricket Club, 74
short runs, 62
Shrewsbury, Arthur, 120
Shropshire, 104–5
signals, umpires', 110
Simpson, 163
Simpson, Reg, 147
single-wicket matches, 33, 85

Skelding, Alex, 126–7, 134, 140, 141, 159
Slindon, 37
Small, John, 51, 53
Smith, E. J., 168
Smith, John, 33
Smith, 'Razor', 128
Smith, Tom, 149
Smithfield, 19
Somerset, 114, 126, 142
South Africa, 129, 144, 148, 150, 153
spectators, 97–8, 117, 159–60
sponsorship, 162
Sporting Life, 113
Sporting Magazine, The, 68, 73, 82
Staffordshire, 89
Star and Garter, 43, 44, 47, 84
staves, umpires', 30–1, 58
Steel, A. G., 121
Stevens, 'Lumpy', 51
Straw, 115
stumps, 32, 51–2
substitutes, 91
Sueter, T., 53, 63
Sunderland Beacon, 77
Surrey, 12, 36–9, 46, 50, 51, 60, 61, 80, 90, 109, 134, 148
Sussex, 25, 38, 50, 51, 71, 78, 104, 126, 133, 134
Swanton, E. W., 146
Swinnocke, George, 18
Sydney, 97–8, 129, 153

Tankerville, Earl of, 54, 63
Tatum, Squire, 46
Taunton, 126
Taylor, Major, 74
Taylor, Tom, 59
tea intervals, 119
telegraph scoring systems, 92
Test and County Cricket Board (TCCB), 158–9
Thesiger, Mr, 91
Thoms, Robert 'Bob', 77, 98–9, 112, 114, 118, 159
three-day matches, 162, 163
thrown out, 32
Tilehurst, 56–7
time-wasting, 163
Times, The, 58–9, 83, 134–5, 158
timing, 125–6
Tomms, Thomas, 65
Transvaal, 153

175

Trent Bridge, 85, 113, 161
Trott, A. E., 134–5
Trueman, Fred, 9
Tufton, J., 60
Tunworth Down, 40
Twyford Down, 86

Uckfield, 101–2
Umpires, clothes of, 22, 58, 89–90,
  101, 121, 123, 164–5
  neutral, 99, 107
  pay, 28–9, 39–40, 87–8
United All England, 101
United States of America, 106

Victoria, 107

Wainwright, Mr, 104–5
Wainwright, Ted, 119–20
Wakeland, Mr, 47
Walker, Tom, 68
Walker brothers, 64
walking, 154–5
Walworth, 46, 82
Ward, William, 70, 91, 116
Ware, 86, 91
Warner, Sir Pelham, 148
Warsoys, Tom, 92
Warwickshire, 119, 168
Waterfall, William, 22
Waymark, Thomas, 40–2
weather, 91, 101–2, 161
Weekes, Everton, 145
Wellington, 166
Wells, John, 58, 60

West, Thomas, 18
West Indies, 129, 156–7, 163–4, 168
  umpiring in, 137–8, 145
Westdean, 37
Westminster school, 83
White, J. C., 126
White, 'Shock', 53–4
White Conduit Club, 43, 47, 66–7
Whitehall Evening Post, 54
Whitehaven, 116–17
wicket-keepers, 45–6
wickets, 32, 70
wides, 74–5, 79
Willes, John, 68, 70–1, 72
Willett pottery collection, 51
Willsher, 80
Winchilsea, Earl of, 56, 67, 69
Windebank, Richard, 86
Windmill Down, 61
Wisden, 96–7
women umpires, 166–7
women's cricket, 10–11, 12–15, 37,
  56, 151–2, 166
Woolley, Frank, 125
Worcester, 144, 148
Worcestershire, 115, 124, 148
World Series Cricket, 151, 164–5
Wright, Peter, 158

Yalden, 63
Yarn, 88–9
Yokohama, 104
York Herald, 88–9
Yorkshire, 125, 138, 160
Yorkshire League, 155